****

ANCIENT
LOVEMAKING SECRETS

-The Journey Toward Immortality-

-

James W. McNeil

Dedication

There are no words in any language that can express the love and gratitude I feel toward my teachers Master Hsu Hong-Chi and Master Chiao Chang-Hung for the many years they spent teaching me and the trust they bestowed upon me in sharing their knowledge. I would also like to thank not only my teachers, but their teachers, and their teachers before them, and Huang-Ti, the Yellow Emperor, for making all this knowledge available.

I am very grateful to the special women in Taiwan for their time, patience, and willingness to help me learn more about myself and more about a woman's feelings, both physical and emotional. Without them my training would never have been completed. I also would like to thank Dagmar Wanke, my number one student in Shih-Shui kung-fu for the many hours she spent editing this book and Michael Ciak for his beautiful illustrations and computer assistance with layout and design.

Acknowledgments

To my family for their patience and to my friends and many students who contributed their time, expertise, support and ideas. Special thanks to:

Paul Abbondante

Larry Amkraut

Keri A. Conoway

Doreen Gagnon

Leo Greenawalt

Sandra Jordan

Mark Komuro

Curtis Wong

TABLE OF CONTENTS

INTRODUCTION

For the past twenty years I have had the great good fortune and honor of being able to study the highest level of kung-fu, the Taoist art of lovemaking. (Most people think of kung-fu as being only fighting, strenuous exercise or only for the young and vigorous person. It's original true meaning was lost many years ago. The term "kung-fu" literally means "hard work" and applies to many practices dedicated to improving health and promoting long life and happiness.) To my knowledge I am the only American student to learn this treasured knowledge directly from Taoist masters in Taiwan. The information I present here is from direct personal experience under the careful guidance of my teachers, Master Hsu Hong-Chi and Master ChiaoChang-Hung.

This training has profoundly changed my life and altered the way I view others. My life is richer than I ever thought possible and I am much more keenly aware of the unhappiness and dissatisfaction felt by others in their lives. Although there remains much for me to learn, I feel that

what I have to share can be of benefit in helping people find the harmony, happiness and satisfaction they long for.

One of the earliest known records of human sexual practices and technique was passed down to us by the Yellow Emperor or Huang-Ti (2698 BC), the father of Chinese civilization. He is credited with having discovered the secret of immortality, or deathless awareness, through the blending of male and female energy during sexual intercourse to produce pure

1

energy and spirit or "shen".

With the help of his advisors, Huang-Ti compiled the "Su Nu Ching" which is a series of questions and answers detailing various aspects of sexual experience. It is a gold mine of original material on ancient Taoist techniques in which sexual energy is utilized to bolster health, develop consciousness and prolong life. It illustrates the essential harmony which exists between men and women through the concept of yin and yang. Men and women are shown to complement each other, neither one being superior over the other.

Yang stands for male, heaven, sun, positive; Yin stands for female, earth, moon, negative. Yang forces are more easily aroused, more active, quicker and stronger than yin. Yin forces are slower to be aroused, calmer in movement and slower to be satisfied. Ultimately, yin is stronger than yang. In the inseparability of these opposites lies the essence of Taoism and the key to immortality.

The ancient Chinese considered the normal human life span to be about one hundred years. According to Taoist wisdom the fact that people deteriorate as early as fifty is due mainly to their lack of understanding of the intrinsic harmony of yin and yang, and their failure to exercise skill and control in lovemaking. The yin-yang element of intercourse must be respected if one wishes to maintain vitality.

Taoism is an ancient philosophy of natural wisdom and perhaps the oldest system of recorded knowledge on earth. The ancient Taoists were very practical in their approach to life in that they did not question the natural order of things, but simply observed and accepted the laws of nature. They were able to acknowledge their own place as human beings in this natural scheme of things and constantly sought ways of meeting human needs in harmony with nature. If a useful technique was found, it would be carefully preserved. The Taoists did not promise that great benefits were to be reaped only after death, but could be gained immediately if certain techniques were practiced correctly.

Modern sexologists and scientists are still learning

much from this ancient wisdom. It is interesting to note also that pornography did not exist in ancient China as sex was never associated with feelings of sin or guilt. It was viewed simply as a way to be in harmony with nature and a way to stay healthy and happy.

The Taoist lovemaking secrets as set forth in Huang-Ti's "Su Nu Ching" continue to be handed down from master to student in the traditional manner to this day, as they were handed to me, and could well be the fountain of youth for many. My purpose in writing this book is to show how men and women can enjoy healthier and happier relationships through exercise, meditation, and skillful lovemaking as taught by Taoists for over 4,000 years.

You will notice throughout this book that emphasis is placed mainly on ways for the man to thoroughly please the woman. This is because a man is generally much easier to satisfy and once he has ejaculated, the lovemaking session is typically over. Women are easily and often left unfulfilled and usually will not speak up for fear of rejection or bruising tender male egos. A woman, when fully satisfied, will give her unconditional love and go to great lengths to please her man. This is a reality of life. However, for lovemaking to successfully reach its full potential, awareness, good intent and effort are required of both partners. Good communication is paramount. If both partners are relaxed and able to freely and openly express their feelings, needs and desires with each other, their lovemaking experience will certainly be a fulfilling one.

It is my sincere hope that after you finish this book you will have a better understanding of sex and its role in creating fulfillment in all aspects of our lives. May you enjoy a lifetime of benefits from what I have learned.

Chapter 1

MY STORY

My life was forever changed in 1976. I was 34 years old and had been involved in kung-fu for ten years, but despite my accomplishments and the relative proficiency of my skill, I knew there was more to learn. I needed to find a teacher who could help me move on to the higher levels in kung-fu. This led me to many different  places and some bitter experiences. However, as with anything else of great value, one cannot expect to find it easily.

In June of that year, my search took me to a kung-fu school in Torrance, California. As I entered the training room I immediately felt an overwhelming sensation that I had found what I was looking for. Strangely, my feelings were not inspired by the surroundings, the students or even the teacher, but by a picture on the wall. It was a photograph of the master, Hsu Hong-Chi (She-Hong-Chee). The benevolent gaze of this man touched me deeply, and spoke to me in a way that I found hard to describe. Although Master Hsu was back in Taiwan, I joined the school that day. I knew it wouldn't be long before I met this remarkable man.

It was Monday, December 3, and there were about twenty students practicing Hsing-I kung-fu the night Master Hsu arrived at the school. We all bowed to him out of respect and when our eyes met, I was again struck by that same feeling I had from the photograph. It was as if I already knew this man, like we had met someplace before. As we continued to practice, Master Hsu made his way around the room watching everyone carefully. Before long he was in front of me, observing and quickly correcting my mistakes.

His visit lasted two months, during which time he often worked with me. I felt that a strong bond was developing between us and although I was sad to see him return to Taiwan, I knew it would be only a matter of time before I would be with him again.

In June of 1977 Master Hsu returned to California. A few weeks after he arrived I was honored to have him as a guest in my own house. This was a rare privilege for me since only senior students are usually accorded such an honor. I was tremendously inspired by his visit during which he not only talked to me about kung-fu, offering his advice and insights, but also took a great interest in my own upbringing. It was during this visit that he confided in me, "From the first night I saw you I knew I had to teach you since I feel we have known each other from another life." When I heard this, everything I had felt previously was con-firmed. The photograph I had seen that first night at the school had indeed spoken to me in some strange way. I felt more strongly than ever that fate had brought me to this man.

Master Hsu told me that I must now train harder than ever; that what was most important was to endure and that I would have to overcome whatever difficulty lay ahead. He let me know that such a road wouldn't be an easy one and that only a person of very strong will and determi-nation would make it through.

Before he returned to Taiwan, he began teaching me a special method of training called Shih Shui (she-sway) kung-fu. This is an ancient and extremely effective system of exercises designed to strengthen the internal organs, increase vitality and develop conciousness. Over time, this training will actually slow the aging process and dramatically enhance immune and sexual functioning.

In mid 1978, Master Hsu wrote to both the senior instructor at the school and me. He invited us to come to Taiwan where we would train and compete in a martial arts tournament. Not long before we were scheduled to leave, the senior instructor decided not to make the trip and forbade any of his students from going as well. I did not question his reasons for not going, however I told him that Master Hsu had personally asked me to go and I was determined to do so. Although I didn't have the money to fund my trip, I had made up my mind to go to Taiwan no matter what it cost me. I sold every item of value I had to raise the money. By making this decision I knew that upon my return to the United States I would no longer be permitted to train at the Torrance kung- fu school.

As I left for Taiwan I was concerned that Grand Master Hsu would most likely assign me to one of his senior instructors, which is the customary practice. To my surprise however, he himself met me at the airport. I was welcomed into his house and stayed with his family. I was even given my own key to the school. For the five weeks I stayed, I trained twelve hours a day, seven days a week. Master Hsu perfected my Hsing-I forms and taught me special chi-kung exercises.

It wasn't until my second visit the following year, in 1979, that Master Hsu formally accepted me as an "indoor" student (a student deemed worthy to receive secret teachings).

A few days after the tournament, we were at the school when Master Hsu invited nine of us to accompany him to a fancy hotel. I had no idea what we were going to do. We went into the room and found it fully stocked with food and liquor and had been there only a short time when there was a knock on the door. Master Hsu opened it and escorted a beautiful young woman into the room. I remember thinking to myself, "What could this beautiful, innocent looking girl possibly want here?" After talking with Master Hsu for a few moments she proceeded to take off her clothes, walk over to one of the Japanese students, unzip his pants and begin to perform oral sex. I couldn't believe it! While this was going on there was another knock on the door and another young woman came into the room and did the same thing. This happened several more times until there were nine women in all. Each woman paired up with a student and found a spot in one of the two bedrooms off the main room, or on the floor.

Master Hsu told each student to enjoy himself, but that he must refrain from ejaculating. He said that if we did ejaculate we would have to sit on the couch and watch as our partner joined another couple. As each student, one by one ended up on the couch, his female partner would join the remaining students, soon resulting in nine women caressing one student. It didn't take long before we all ended up on the couch.

At first Master Hsu became angry. He told us to begin again and not to ejaculate. Soon we were all sitting on the couch again. He was furious at our lack of control and berated each one of us. He then got on the bed and began to make love with all nine women to show us that it was possible to do so without ejaculating. This lasted for at least an hour. When we left the hotel it was 5:30 a.m.

Master Hsu told us to go home and rest and that he would see us again later in the day. The other students went to their rooms to sleep but I headed for the kung-fu school to begin another grueling day of training. This was just the first of what would be many nights of going without sleep followed by a full day of kung-fu training. Although I had not realized it at the time, that first night at the hotel had been my introduction to the Taoist art of lovemaking.

That afternoon Master Hsu and I were having lunch at a restaurant when he told me of his feelings for me as a student and how he felt compelled to teach me. "Our ties run beyond this world, for we have met before and that meeting has drawn us together again. You train hard now, but you must train harder than everyone else if you want to be good. I only hope you will never let me down for it has happened many times before." He then offered to teach me the highest level of kung-fu, Taoist Lovemaking: the art of

8

loving, controlling ejaculation and cultivating sexual energy. He explained that the system had been handed down secretly for thousands of years through the works of Huang-Ti the Yellow Emperor. Master Hsu went on to say that many people claim to have learned the art of lovemaking, but that their knowledge came strictly from books, not direct instruction, and that traditionally, a teacher will pass this information in its entirety to only one student. He decided to pass his knowledge of this system on to me if I committed myself to learning it.

This was one of the highest honors that could be bestowed upon any Chinese student, but for it to be given to an American student was unheard of. Master Hsu often liked to tell me that I was only "American on the outside and Chinese on the inside." I did not hesitate to accept his offer to teach me. Overcome with emotion, tears came to my eyes as I nodded my head and said "Thank-you, Master."

The following day he took me to another hotel. "For the next four weeks," he said, "You will not be allowed to ejaculate in any way at any time. You will be making love to different women. These women will be your tools for enlightenment. You might think that this training is going to be fun, easy and exciting but you are wrong. At first it will be hard work, harder than you can ever imagine. If you try to cheat or lie to me I will know, and you will never learn anything from me again. Don't disappoint me. Make me proud of you and I will pass on to you the secret of immortality, the knowledge of the Taoist internal elixir that so many try to achieve. People can read about these things in books, but you will be experiencing them first hand! It won't be easy, but when you are through it will be worth more to you than all the money in the world." At Master Hsu's request I promised not to tell anyone about what I was learning until such time as he gave me permission or until after his death.

While we were talking a young Chinese woman, Yo-Eko, arrived. Master Hsu said a few words to her in Chinese then turned to me and said, "Your training will begin with learning how to hold, touch, feel and kiss - acts

9

most people take for granted." I was instructed on how to feel with my lips, hands, body and mind. Neither of us were allowed to take off our clothes. We practiced each aspect over and over again.

For the next two days, we repeated each stage of the training; holding, feeling and caressing with great care and attention. Finally, I was allowed to slowly unbutton her blouse and take off her clothes, all the time kissing, holding and touching with intense feeling. Throughout this entire time I was not allowed to touch her breasts or remove her underwear. She was very beautiful and her body was flawless. I could barely contain myself. The time seemed to stretch on endlessly as I continued to kiss and caress this beautiful woman. I was ready to explode, but I could do nothing to relieve myself. I had given my word to my teacher. Slowly I began to gain control over my emotions and kept my mind from focusing on my aroused penis - a task not easily accomplished under the circumstances.

On the third day I was allowed to take off her underwear and to touch her breasts and her vagina - a procedure that was again to be repeated many times and always with great care and attention. It was only after we had practiced this for a couple of hours that Master Hsu told me that I could slide my penis into her vagina. Yo-Eko shifted her hips as I slowly penetrated her. It felt so good going inside her! Master Hsu was always standing right there beside us, sometimes guiding my hips with his hands and reminding me to go slowly and use the techniques he had taught me. But, it was too much for me to handle, I was going to ejaculate so I quickly pulled out. That first day I pulled out many times, I couldn't stay inside her for more than a minute or two. My teacher kept saying, "Take your mind out of your penis and put it in your head where it belongs!" We stopped and started many times that day.

The next day we started over again from the beginning -holding, touching, kissing, slowly taking off her clothes and finally, slowly penetrating. I was doing better. Then Master Hsu taught me a new technique called "nine shallow one deep." I concentrated on following his directions for thrusting inside her, continuously repeating the

10

pattern of nine shallow thrusts and then one deep thrust, nine shallow and then one deep. Then I lost my concentration for a moment. I began to feel myself getting out of control as my body moved faster and faster. Master Hsu caught me and suddenly I felt a sharp slap on my rear, the pain of which ripped through my entire body. He yelled, "Not yet stupid, learn to control!" Practicing this over and over again was almost more than I could bear. I wanted to scream out, "Just let me finish one time, please!"

I never thought I would make it through that day without ejaculating. Lying in bed that night, my penis was as hard as a rock and I badly wanted to masturbate. I thought to myself, "Go ahead, he will never find out." But I had made a promise to my teacher and that promise, in spite of my discomfort, meant more to me than a few seconds of pleasure.

The weeks passed by as I moved from one phase of the training to the next. At first I had difficulty comprehending everything he was trying to teach me, but I kept working harder and harder as the time was growing near for my return to the United States. I had also fallen in love with Yo-Eko, which Master Hsu had cautioned me to avoid. After I returned to California I wrote to her each month telling her how I felt about her, how beautiful she was and how I would get back to Taiwan as quickly as I could.

The following year, in October, I was back in Taiwan for my third visit. I continued my intensive training at the kung-fu school, from 6:00-11:30 am, but when I was not training, I was thinking constantly about Yo-Eko. I was anxious to be with her again. Master Hsu seemed to know what was on my mind, and when we finally went to the hotel he had a surprise for me. "This is your new partner," he said as he introduced me to another young woman. "Her name is Mei-Tsu." When he saw the look on my face he said, "You are here to learn Taoist Lovemaking, something very few people have the chance to learn and you want to throw it away over a girl you knew for only a few weeks. Many people's lives have been destroyed over what they think is love, but what is in fact only lust. You are still a baby as far as this is concerned and you need to grow up.

Now do you want to continue and show me what you have learned or do you want to see Yo-Eko?"

My heart sank. I told him that I wanted to learn, but inside I was consumed with the desire to be with Yo-Eko. I tried to comfort myself with the thought that I could contact her later on, but just then Master Hsu, as if reading my mind said, "You will not write to her or see her again, do you understand?" I was heartbroken. Why was he doing this to me? I almost told him that I wanted to be with her, but I thought better of it and told him that I wanted to learn and grow up and promised that I would not see her again. It was a bitter moment for me.

So I started training with Mei-Tsu. She was also beautiful, about twenty, with long black hair and a perfect body. We started practicing everything I had been taught before. Master Hsu continued to correct my mistakes as we went along and I suddenly felt that I hadn't learned anything. I became frustrated and annoyed with myself. This woman was so different in every way from Yo-Eko; her movements, her wants and needs. It was as if I was learning all over again. The kissing, touching and feeling were there, only it didn't work in the same way with Mei-Tsu as it had with Yo-Eko.

When we returned home Master Hsu was angry. We talked for a couple of hours and he reminded me of why I was in Taiwan and that the learning would not be easy. "Take your brains out of your penis and put them back into your head where they belong. It's up to you. Either do that or don't bother trying to learn." That night I walked through the streets thinking of Yo-Eko and about everything that had happened, trying to decide what I was going to do. Although I missed and felt I truly loved Yo-Eko very much and wanted to be with her, I didn't want to disappoint my teacher as he had put so much trust in me. What was I to do?

Early the next morning I began training harder than ever to try to forget about Yo-Eko. Master Hsu came in and when he looked at me I think he knew what I had decided upon. I wanted to please my teacher and make him proud of me. I wanted to prove to him that he had chosen the right

12

person and to let him know that I would never let him down. He stayed to watch me train for an hour without saying a word. Then at 11:30 he told me to clean up so we could eat lunch. During the meal he did not utter a word. I was concerned that he may have changed his mind about teaching me. Finally, I broke the silence by saying, "Master, I am sorry, please give me another chance." He looked up at me and said quietly, "I know."

A couple of days later we went to the hotel and waited for Mei-Tsu. When she arrived she seemed different in a way I found difficult to describe. She was more fun-loving and cheerful, as if she too had made some decision. We began the training again while Master Hsu watched, correcting my mistakes, offering encouragement and making sure that I wasn't losing control. I had to stop several times as I came close to the point of no return. Mei-Tsu seemed to think it was funny, but I wasn't laughing because it was hard work. But I knew she wasn't really laughing at me as she was keenly aware of what I was going through and how difficult it really was. In only the few short hours I had known her, I was beginning to develop strong feelings toward Mei- Tsu also, but told myself that it was only lust, as Master Hsu suggested. On the way home Master Hsu turned to me and asked if I had learned something today. I nodded, "Yes Sir, thank you. I learned that one should not mistake lust for love."

We continued to train almost every day. During the last week before I was to return home, Master Hsu said I was going to learn something a little different. He took me over to meet Mei-Tsu and this time, another woman was with her too. It was time for the next step. I was anxious to start and was becoming increasingly more aroused as we talked about what we would be doing.

Mei-Tsu and I began kissing slowly, but her girl-friend May-Hwa interrupted us and asked me to kiss her. When I did, I noticed she was kissing differently. May-Hwa turned to Master Hsu and said, "He is kissing wrong. He is kissing like a man kisses a woman, not like a woman kisses a woman. There isn't enough feeling in his kisses." She began to show me how to kiss using Mei-Tsu as her partner.

13

It looked so sensuous and beautiful. I practiced with both of them again and again, and watched the two of them together as they taught me the technique of two women touching and kissing. I had to copy the way they moved their bodies, tongues and hands, and the feeling they put behind it.

They taught me to make love to every part of a woman's body like a woman would make love to another woman. May-Hwa taught me how to kiss Mei-Tsu's vagina and clitoris, showing me how to position my hands and use different methods such as blowing and variations of tongue movements. Each technique brought her a different level of orgasm, each one more intense than the previous one.

I began to kiss May-Hwa, slowly working my way down to her vagina. The angle of her vagina was different than Mei-Tsu's, therefore so were the ways in which it could be stimulated. I had to use different variations of the techniques she had taught me to use on Mei-Tsu. We continued in this way for the rest of my stay in Taiwan.

At times I would be overwhelmed by my emotions and would have to stop for a while to regain my composure. By making love with two women at the same time I learned how to satisfy the very different needs of each one. It was a very important learning experience for me.

Back in the States I practiced everything I had learned; controlling ejaculation, touching, holding, feeling, kissing and most of all how "to keep my brains out of my penis." I knew Master Hsu would have something special to teach me when I returned to Taiwan for the fourth time and I wanted to be prepared. I practiced harder to perfect everything he had taught me in both martial arts and love-making. This time my desire was not for Yo-Eko or Mei-Tsu, but to make my teacher proud of me.

That summer Master Hsu came to my home in California to continue my training and in October of 1981 I returned to Taiwan where he again met me at the airport. It was good to see him. He asked if I had been practicing and I told him I had been doing my best to practice what he had taught me.

I continued to train with my kung-fu brothers at the

school and on my fourth day there, Master Hsu resumed my lovemaking training. He took me to a new hotel where a woman named Ting-Ting was waiting for us. I was to make love with her and to satisfy her. Master Hsu said that she specialized in a technique that I would find out about later.

Ting-Ting and I stood up together. I held her hand and pulled her toward me gently. I took my time and made love to her slowly. We made love for nearly three hours. Master Hsu observed every move I made and finally stopped us when it was time to go and to tell me he was pleased. On our way home Master Hsu said, "Tomorrow you will learn that special technique with Ting-Ting's help." I was definitely curious.

The next day Master Hsu taught me how to practice controlling erections. When he said "down" I was to bring it down and when he said "up" I was to bring it up. This continued throughout our lovemaking session. As Ting-Ting began kissing my penis, Master Hsu said "Down!" I looked at him and then at my penis in Ting-Ting's mouth. It would not go down. He yelled again, "I said down, now!" Ting-Ting was doing her best to keep it from going down. If this was a contest, she was winning.

My teacher yelled again, louder this time, "Down! Now! Down! Down!" Ting-Ting was smiling; she loved a challenge, but when Master Hsu yelled at me like that I got scared and started to lose my erection. Ting-Ting continued working my penis and it started to come up again. "I didn't say up yet!" yelled Master Hsu, "Get down!" This went on

and on for what felt like days. I don't know what was harder, learning to control my ejaculation or my erection. It took three weeks of daily practice to master this technique.

During my last week in Taiwan Master Hsu had me training with Ting-Ting and three other women, each of whom was a specialist in a certain technique. One day, rather than go to a hotel as we had been doing, we went to a secluded house in the mountains. I felt that this was going to be a special day and I was right.

After about forty-five minutes of driving through the scenic mountains of Taiwan, we arrived at a beautiful Chinese style house perched on a hillside. We walked up and knocked at the door where an older woman of about fifty-five answered and let us in. She introduced herself as Yu- Lin and led us into a large room overlooking the picturesque valley. The tea was already on the table.

I was struck by how powerful and wise she seemed when she spoke to me, "Your teacher thinks very highly of you and feels you should be handed the secrets of Taoist Lovemaking. You are very fortunate to have been chosen to receive this knowledge. We have known your teacher for many years and it has always been understood that when he finds a student whom he finds worthy, we would teach him, but only if that student has successfully past certain tests. You, I understand, have done that or you would not be here". By the time we finished our tea, my anticipation was very great.

We walked into an elegantly furnished bedroom where Yu-Lin introduced me to Su-Ling, Chu-Mei and Ting-Ting whom, of course, I already knew. Yu-Lin and Master Hsu sat against the wall and instructed me to go take a shower with the three women. Once we were finished we returned to the bedroom and started kissing and caressing each other. I was very aroused when Master Hsu suddenly said, "Make your penis go down." I succeeded in doing this as the girls continued kissing and fondling me in every way. I was enjoying the delights of kissing Su-Ling's lovely vagina, when Yu-Lin interrupted by saying, "Ok, now let me see it go up." This up and down practice had gone on for about half an hour when Master Hsu and Yu-Lin nodded their approval and left, but not without reminding me not to ejaculate. Yu-Lin said in Chinese, "Do your best, girls!" They giggled and said, "Yes ma'am!"

We were left alone for the next three hours during which time Su-Ling, Chu-Mei and Ting-Ting each taught me different ways to satisfy a woman.

When Yu-Lin and Master Hsu came back we were

still making love and "learning." At that point we stopped and I got dressed. Yu-Lin said, "We will teach you many things in addition to helping you enhance and improve what you already know. But remember, the things you learn here should never be taught to anyone except to those students whom you deem worthy. We will show you how to teach a woman to make love to a man and how to control and direct the sexual energy generated during lovemaking. You will learn how to give a woman the ultimate gift of total orgasm. These next few days will truly be a learning experience that you will never forget. Go home and rest now. Tomorrow when you come back we will continue with your training."

The next day I was waiting outside contemplating the beautiful mountains when Yu-Lin came and told me it was time to meet with Chu-Mei. She was the quietest of the three girls. Yu-Lin explained that she would teach me about a deeper kind of lovemaking that most people don't understand. "She spends most of her time meditating and mind traveling, but still enjoys physical lovemaking once in a while. Spiritual lovemaking and cultivating sexual energy are what she enjoys best. She is also a very psychic person, as you will soon find out. I will be translating for her as she speaks only Taiwanese."

She led me to Chu-Mei's room, but just before we got there we heard the sounds of a mantra being spoken. Yu-Lin said that we would have to wait for a little while as Chu-Mei was still in meditation. I went back outside to wait, and a short while later Yu-Lin came and told me that it was time, she was finished.

As we entered her room the first thing I noticed was a beautiful large altar made of dark teak wood. Chu-Mei was standing there waiting for us. We sat down and she served us some tea. Chu-Mei said something and Yu-Lin translated it as: "Chu-Mei said she was sorry keeping us waiting". I told her, "Do not be sorry as it is an honor that you are even seeing me, and I am the one who is sorry for bothering you." Chu-Mei said, "You are very kind." As Yu-Lin translated she spoke slowly to make sure I understood everything. Chu-Mei continued, "I am going to be very honest with you. The first time I was asked to teach

17

you, I refused. However, Ting-Ting had good things to say about you and Madam Yu believed in Master Hsu's decision to give you the knowledge of the higher levels of lovemaking. When I first saw you, when Madam Yu brought you into the master bedroom that first day, I noticed there seemed to be a glow about you, you walked proud but humble. Then I was not sure if I would teach you, but in the last few days I have learned to know everything about you. You are an honest, sincere, kind and humble person and you have power that even you do not know you have. Many people will respect you and many will take advantage of you. I now understand why Master Hsu and Madam Yu want me to teach you.

One day after Master Hsu passes away you will find another teacher whose knowledge is far more advanced than any other teacher in Taiwan. This teacher will teach you many things from where I leave off. Even this teacher does not know today that you will be his student in a few years. Then, if you continue to practice hard, you will be tested and if you pass, you will meet your last teacher, a teacher not from this world. This teacher will lead you toward immortality. This is all truth and one day you will know. The things I am going to teach you will include cultivation of sexual energy, mind travel and much more. I will give you the basic tools to train, but you must practice as much as you can."

For two days we trained together and I was introduced to the secrets of spiritual lovemaking and cultivating sexual energy. We trained ten hours a day together. On the last day just before I left Chu-Mei said, "One day we will meet again, but in the spirit world. Please train hard." This was a very profound experience for me and I regret that I cannot divulge any detailed information about the training at this time.

In all I spent six days with the women at the mountain retreat to practice and learn and after that I never saw them again. I was sad to leave them as we had become very close and had shared something very fine and beautiful.

After we left Master Hsu told me, "What you have learned these past few days from these women and all that you have learned in the years before should never be forgotten. Now you can understand why Huang-Ti, The Yellow Emperor, had three female advisors, Plain Girl, Mysterious Girl and Rainbow Girl, to teach him about sexual matters. One day you will find a student who is worthy of this knowledge and you must then pass it on so it will never die." I felt very lucky and a little overwhelmed by the responsibility implied in being the holder of this amazing knowledge. I was also beginning to realize the full impact that the Shih-Shui training and the Taoist Lovemaking training was having on me. Like the Yellow Emperor of long ago, I too was developing a means of actually controlling all the functions of my body and strengthening it internally.

In the summer of 1982 Master Hsu came to California and stayed at my house again. He gave a couple of seminars with some of his old students and taught at my kung-fu school. In the evenings he and I would stay up, sometimes all night, to talk about many things. He told many stories about his life and training in Taiwan and he taught me about fighting, acupressure and Tui-Na (bonesetting and healing). And of course, we would go over everything I had learned about lovemaking and the importance of it.

That fall, in October, I returned to Taiwan for a kung-fu tournament and Master Hsu and I again spent a lot of time together. This time he did not teach me lovemaking with any of the girls but used the time to teach me other things. In the mornings we would often take a taxi up the mountain to an area where many other people gathered to practice their various disciplines. He would correct my kung-fu while chatting with his many friends there.

In January of 1984, during the Chinese New Year celebration, I was back in Taiwan again for three weeks and saw Master Hsu many times. It was also then that I was first introduced to Master Chiao Chang-Hung, the most respected kung-fu master in martial arts today. It was he who brought the Shih-Shui system from China to Taiwan and had taught Master Hsu's teacher.

I was back in California when on October 9, 1984, I received a phone call from Taiwan informing me that Master Hsu had died unexpectedly. I left right away for the funeral.

While there, I again met with Master Chiao. He could see how much Master Hsu had meant to me and was impressed that I had come all the way back to Taiwan on such short notice. It was then that he accepted me as his first American student.

Master Chiao is the 33rd generation master of the oldest Taoist kung-fu system known today, Little Nine Heaven Wu Tao kung-fu, which includes the Shih-Shui internal training. He is also a master of Pa-kua and Hsing-I, as well as Meditation, Dual Cultivation and Levitation. I have been a student of Master Chiao's now since 1984 and am learning the higher levels of Dual Cultivation, Shih-Shui, Acupressure, Pa-kua and Little Nine Heaven Wu Tao.

I will always be grateful for being led to the path which took me to Taiwan and to the remarkable teachers I have been fortunate enough to study with over the past twenty years.

Chapter 2

THE BASICS

Breathing

One of the first things that I had to learn when I started studying the internal styles of kung- fu was to start breathing through the "tan-tien." The term tan-tien, literally translates from Chinese as "field of elixir." It is an area of the body capable of generating and storing "chi", or energy, and is located 3 inches below and 3 inches in from the navel. At first it was hard for me to break my life-long habits of breathing, but I practiced every day and soon it became natural. In regards to this type of training the Chinese say "You should come back younger," and "Make the unnatural natural again." Little did I know this lesson in breathing was my first step toward my destiny in learning the highest level of kung-fu, the treasured art of Taoist lovemaking.

Breathing is considered the most important function of the body because all other functions depend upon it. We can exist for some time without eating, and a shorter time without water, but without breathing, our existence is measured by minutes. It is the first thing given to us and the last thing taken away. We tend to take breathing for granted, even while knowing it is keeping us alive.

Through the stress of modern daily life, many of us have forgotten how to breathe correctly. Notice how an infant's little stomach goes in and out as he breathes. The stomach will expand on inhalation, and contract on exhalation. Who taught this little infant to breathe? No one did; it is the natural way to breathe. If you look in his mouth while he is sleeping, you will also see that the tongue is gently touching the roof of the mouth, the natural way.

The Taoists believe that we should work at becoming younger and change back to our inborn way of doing things so we can live a long and healthy life. This is obtainable by doing chi- kung exercises, beginning with proper breathing.We go to various health clubs to tone our external bodies so we can look good, but seldom do we give a thought about toning our internal organs. Special breathing exercises can greatly improve the health and strength of our organs and their ability to keep us healthy and free of disease.

Breathing is basic to the life of our physical body. Not only does it keep us alive, but it is used to move into many different states of consciousness and levels of energy. The cycle of inhalation and exhalation mirrors the principle of yin and yang and forms a link between human beings and spiritual energies.

The Taoists teach several different breathing methods. The method most commonly used is "natural" breathing. To do this, simply breathe in a natural relaxed way allowing the tongue to touch the roof of the mouth and without forcing the air in. This opens the energy channels or "meridians" and allows the chi to circulate freely.

The next method of breathing is used to move chi from the tan-tien into the meridians. By relaxing the abdominal muscles and literally pushing the breath down into the pelvis, the flow of chi is greatly enhanced. The important thing is to focus your attention on the tan-tien. The anal sphincter must be slightly closed yet relaxed to allow the energy to move up through the eight psychic meridians, which I will later describe in more detail. Relaxed muscles allow energy to circulate smoothly.

It is very important to understand that Taoist exercises in general are easy and natural to do and that the primary concern is for health and longevity.

The following diagrams illustrate three kinds of breathing:

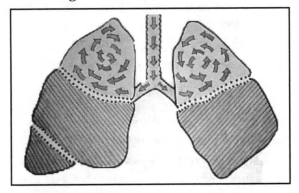

1. Upper breathing in which only one-third of the lungs is being used.

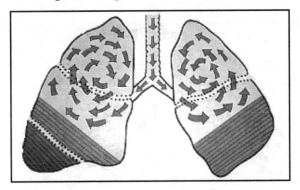

2. Middle breathing in which only two-thirds of the lungs is being used.

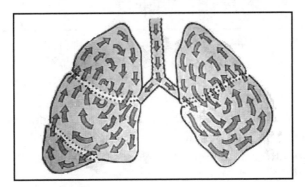

3. Complete breathing in which the total lung capacity is being used.

We are meant to breathe the third way, as we all did when we were babies. Only with complete breathing can all the stagnant air be removed from the bottom of our lungs and be replaced with fresh air.

The following exercise will show you the way to proper breathing using the entire lung. This will assist in keeping you more relaxed and healthy.

First, touch your tongue lightly to the roof of your mouth, and close your mouth gently. Inhale in a relaxed way through your nose down to your tan-tien. Your stomach will expand as you inhale and contract as you exhale. Place your hands on your stomach so that you can feel this happening and to remind yourself that you should always breathe this way.

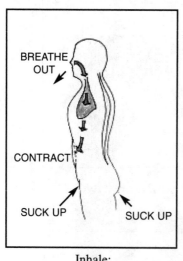

Inhale:
the stomach
expands

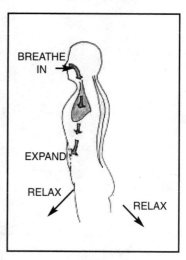

Exhale:
the stomach
contracts

Practice this method of breathing frequently until it becomes a habit. Be sure not to inhale and exhale through your mouth. Breathe through your nose and keep the chest relaxed.

24

Meditation

Meditation has been common practice within many cultures for thousands of years. It is well known that people who meditate on a regular basis typically have lower blood pressure and live longer than those who don't. They also enjoy more moments of serenity, enhanced mental capacity and functioning and reduced stress. Regular meditation can definitely help in your love life. By learning to empty your mind and find harmony within yourself you will better be able to enjoy the benefits of sexual spontaneity. You will be able to transcend fixed expectations in lovemaking and approach your partner with openness and harmony.

There are many different techniques of meditation from basic breathing to meditation that cultivates energy through the movement of chi in your body. You can also learn meditation techniques with a partner that will allow you to cultivate chi in both your bodies.

A basic form of meditation and one of the easiest ways to empty your mind, is to count each complete cycle of inhalation and exhalation while breathing.

Sit comfortably on a firm cushion with your legs crossed, in lotus position, or straight out in front of you. What is most important is that you are comfortable. Keep your spine straight and your eyes slightly closed. Relax and breathe through your nose counting the cycles of your breathing up to one hundred or more. Think only of your breathing. Slowly, let your mind empty of everyday thoughts. Focus your attention inwardly. If a thought disturbs you or your mind begins to wander, simply notice this and begin counting again.

Remember that learning to empty your mind is achieved only through continual practice. Do not let yourself get discouraged too easily, the results are well worth pursuing.

After mastering this method of meditation, begin to place your focus on your tan-tien. By concentrating on this area you will be able to achieve a settled state of inner wakefulness without the conscious effort of counting your breath. Maintaining this inner wakefulness will help you to eliminate deep rooted stress and begin the process of self-realization. You will become one with yourself as your awareness of body and mind integrate.

Remember that meditation should be practiced regularly, every day if possible. When Master Chiao first introduced me to meditation, he explained to me these things I should remember:

- Relax completely with your eyes slightly closed.
- Do not eat before meditation.
- Sit up straight on the edge of a hard pad.
- Put your tongue at the roof of your mouth.
- Concentrate on the tan-tien while trying to eliminate any thoughts from your brain.
- The best time is first thing in the morning and/or before going to bed.
- Meditate for as long as you are comfortable starting with at least 15 minutes to 30 minutes.

After about fifteen minutes certain physical sensations may appear such as heat, cold or tingling depending on your level of meditation. This will most likely happen first at the center of the hands and then in the tan-tien.

The practice of meditation will allow you to quiet your mind and observe the true nature of self. This in turn will allow you to slowly access the vast realm of untapped capabilities we possess as human beings.

What is Chi?

Chi is the energy that flows through the human body. It is the vitality or "life force" that keeps us alive. In an effort to find some pragmatic explanation for this phenomenon and after centuries of observation and practice, the ancient Taoist masters found ways to measure and manipulate chi. It was found that by stimulating one part of the body with pressure, heat, cold or the insertion of needles, another seemingly unrelated part of the body could be significantly affected.

Various exercises were then developed which could affect the quantity and intensity of chi. It was further observed that chi traveled along specific, consistent pathways through the different body parts and internal organs. Entire systems of these pathways called meridians, which govern the flow of chi, were mapped out in great detail. These are fundamental to the now highly sophisticated healing arts of acupuncture and acupressure from which many people gain great benefit today. Despite many attempts by Western scientists to rationalize these observations, the flow of chi through these meridians bears no relationship to the human nervous or circulatory systems.

Chi, then, is used to describe the energy that holds our organs in place, regulates our body temperature, and generally serves to maintain most of our bodily functions. Scientists know it exists because they can interrupt, enhance, or change its flow. Many say chi can be compared to the concept of electricity which is almost impossible to properly describe. Nevertheless, scientists can clearly show that electricity exists because it can cause extreme consequences when touched. It can be measured. It can run electric motors. It can have high or low voltage. It can be magnified by certain actions and it can be impeded. As with electricity, chi is mostly described by its properties or consequences. Chi continues to defy attempts to dissect it in laboratories and to physically see it. It just is. This is a simple matter of fact for the Taoist, but can be maddening to the Western mind. There are three sources of chi: **Original Chi, Grain Chi** and **Natural Air Chi**.

Original Chi is different for everyone and can greatly vary in power and intensity from person to person. It is transmitted from parent to child at conception and stored in the kidneys. There is nothing humans can do to affect the amount or intensity of Original Chi that comes to them. However, each person has the ability to develop it to its fullest extent through special chi- kung exercises and good health habits or to destroy it through careless behavior.

The energy that comes from food and assists people in activating and developing the full potential of their Original Chi is called **Grain Chi**.

The final source of chi comes from the air we breathe. Taoists found that regardless of how strong Original Chi may be or how carefully one balanced a diet with Grain Chi, nobody could attain their full potential without **Natural Air Chi**. Natural Air Chi is extracted from the air through the lungs. Consequently, in Taoist systems of health and in the martial arts, great emphasis is placed on methods of breathing. Without proper breathing one risks a shrinkage of Original Chi.

Increasing Chi Through Meditation

After I had learned sitting meditation, Master Chiao taught me how to circulate chi through my body. This continuous flow of energy in a single circuit is called the "Hsiao Chow-Tien" or "Little Nine Heaven Circle".

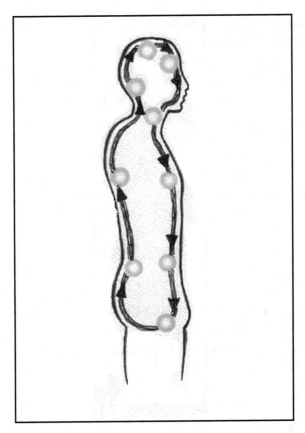

The "Nine Little Heavens" are at the crown, between the eyes, throat, heart, tan-tien, Huei-yin point (see p. 41), coccyx, middle of back and base of skull.

Centuries ago the Taoists discovered that there are two main energy channels within the body. The first is the Governor, or Yang channel which starts at the Huei-yin point, located at the perineum (see pg. #40) and flows upward into the tail bone, up through the spine and into the base of the skull. From there it enters the brain and then moves downward to the roof of the mouth.

The second channel is called the Functional, or Yin channel. This channel connects with its opposite, the Governor channel, at the roof of the mouth through the throat to the heart. From the heart the energy flows through the abdominal organs and back down to the perineum.

In order to maintain a continuous circuit, it is very important to meditate with the tongue pressed lightly to the roof of the mouth. By doing so, one is able to provide a bridge for energy to travel from the roof of the mouth to the lower front of the body.

Master Chiao explained, "When you are beginning to practice this form of meditation, try to focus your mind on the two channels. Inhale and visualize the energy flowing up the Governor channel. Exhale and the energy will flow down the Functional channel. At first one must visualize the chi flowing through the channels, but after a while it will flow naturally. With practice you will be able to circulate your chi at any time, any place and under any conditions."

After practicing the Little Nine Heaven circulation for a year, Master Chiao taught me how to circulate energy through the "Eight Psychic Meridians." This meditation was much more involved and moved chi throughout all of my body. He said to start off with the Little Nine Heaven circulation for about ten minutes and then start the Eight Psychic Meridians:

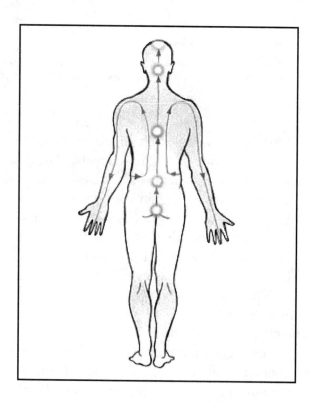

Inhale and bring the energy up the Governor
Meridian from the perineum or Huei-Yin
Point to the top of the head.

Exhale and bring the energy down the Functional
Meridian to the Huei-Yin Point (as in the
Little Nine Heaven circulation).

Inhale and bring the energy up to the navel, around
the Belt Meridian to the sides of the back,
then up the sides of the back to the
shoulders.

Exhale moving the energy down the outer sides of
both arms to the hands then over the end of
the middle finger to the palm of each hand.

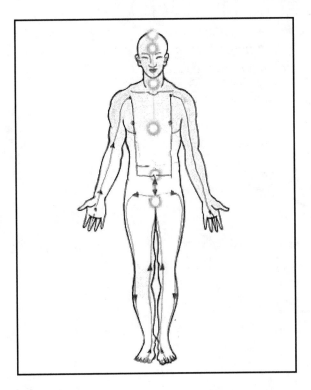

Inhale up the inner sides of both arms to the chest.

Exhale and the energy comes down both sides of
the chest, back to the belt meridian, across to
the belly button, and down to the Huei-Yin.

Inhale and bring the energy up to the solar
plexus.

Exhale and go back down to the Huei-Yin then
across and down the outer sides of both legs,
over the end of the middle toe to the middle
of the ball of the foot.

Inhale up the inner sides of both legs to the Huei-
Yin, then up to the Tan-Tien.

Exhale to the Huei-Yin then start over again.

*As a general rule, energy moves up on the inhale
and down on the exhale.*

Increasing Chi Through Back-to-Back Meditation

After I had mastered the Little Nine Heaven circulation successfully, Master Chiao said I should start to practice back-to-back meditation with a partner. "By practicing this way you and your partner will be able to combine your chi within each other's bodies."

He grabbed a firm straw pad, placed it on the floor between us and said, "You and I will sit here back to back. Remember to keep your tongue on the roof of your mouth. Breath naturally and soon your breath will regulate to mine. We will both focus our minds on the chi of each other. Begin to feel my chi. Let your mind guide the chi as it flows through the Little Nine Heaven circle and combines with mine at the base of our spines and flows up the Governor channel. Allow the chi to flow at will without forcing it. The movement of your chi is totally within the power of your mind."

We practiced this form of meditation for a few hours every day while I was in Taiwan. He explained that it allows you to cultivate chi to higher levels than previously experienced. At advanced levels chi is circulated through the Eight Psychic Meridians.

The following year when Master Chiao came to the United States, he taught me Pa-kua and Little Nine Heaven Kung-Fu and we practiced back-to-back meditation daily. We also talked about many things; his life at the temple, his teachers, and what he expected of me. He told me that if I practiced hard, I too would one day be able to reach very advanced levels of meditation. He went on to say that he felt when the time was right I would have one more teacher and that I had the capability of one day achieving immortality. But this could only happen if I continued to meditate regularly and trained hard, as there was always more learn.

I asked him, "But what is immortality?"

"An immortal is one who has undergone difficult training because he believed in the Tao and its teachings and has committed to live well the full span of his life. An immortal is that person who has attained an eternal life, has shed all human emotions and all ambitions of fame and glory; he will be free from death as we see it. Take Tao not so much as a religion, but as a way of life. You must gain control over all aspects of your self including your sexual desires and this can be done by practicing chi-kung exercises and meditation.

There are many different forms of chi-kung exercises. If practiced correctly, they will help one achieve a balance of yin and yang, which in turn will build up the three energies of ching, chi and shen which will produce pure spirit and then, emptiness."

"But what are ching, chi and shen? I don't understand."

"Ching is your sexual essence, chi is your breath and shen is your mind. You must learn to transfer your ching to chi, transfer your chi to shen, and cultivate shen so it returns to the state of emptiness or 'shu.'

You can find a woman who accepts the way of Tao and if you and she can empty all your sexual desires of lust and practice sexual meditation while circulating the chi through the eight psychic meridians, then you both will be on the right road to achieving the immortal body of Tao."

Then one day he told me he was going to teach me an advanced method of meditation; meditation I would share with a woman.

He said, "This style of sexual meditation will also be done back-to-back. You will have to put your spirit inside the woman and guide it to different parts of her body. In this way she can have an orgasm without the physical touch of lovemaking."

My partner, Melinda, wanted very much to practice this style of meditation. So Master Chiao agreed to teach her as well.

Melinda and I practiced every day for a month, but neither of us really felt anything dramatic. Then a few days later Melinda orgasmed. She collapsed in ecstacy and whispered, "It was just like having an orgasm but without having sex. It was the most beautiful thing I have ever experienced." We practiced back-to-back as often as we could. She loved to feel my energy flow through her body.

I didn't practice this style of meditation with any other woman until August 1992 when a student named Lindsey whose kung-fu had become very good wanted to learn back-to-back sexual meditation. Over the next month we practiced many times but I had never gone inside Lindsey with my spirit even though she had asked many times. One night I decided I would. I sent my spirit inside her body, and kept it there for twenty-five minutes. She shuffled to the side and collapsed whispering, "It was so beautiful, thank you." Later, she told her roommate that she just had her most powerful orgasm and that she did it without having sex or even touching herself.

Chapter 3

INCREASING STRENGTH & POWER IN MEN

In June of 1977 when Master Hsu first came to my home, he taught me special chi-kung exercises to help me control ejaculation and to strengthen all my internal organs. He said they originated from Huang-Ti the Yellow Emperor and that a Taoist priest had passed them on to him. He told me, "If you can practice these exercises for at least one year, your abdomen will become very strong. Your physical strength will increase to a very remarkable degree and during sexual intercourse, you will be able to maintain an erection for a long time. Be sure to concentrate on your abdomen while doing the deep breathing."

In 1984, Master Chiao taught me the same exercises along with others, elaborating on their importance. Most of the exercises, some of which I will give in the next section, are directed at strengthening the pelvic floor muscles and the kidneys.

Strengthening the Pubococcygeus or PC muscle (part of a group of muscles that run from the pubic bone to the tail bone) is essential as it is fundamental to healthy sexual functioning for both men and women. Poor muscle tone in this area can lead to sexual difficulties and other problems. Contracting this muscle during lovemaking will greatly enhance your pleasure.

In regards to human sexuality, the Chinese believe that the kidneys are the most important organs in the human body. Most people with sexual problems have weak kidneys and therefore they lack energy. Sometimes, after a man has an ejaculation his kidneys or lower back will become sore.

The following exercises will help to relieve and prevent these backaches in addition to strengthening the kidneys. By doing these simple exercises every day a man can actually increase his hormone levels and improve blood circulation. Regular practice will help him improve and maintain his sexual powers and youthful organs by increasing the power of the testicles and pelvic floor muscles. Do not underestimate these exercises. They are very simple and easy to do and will strengthen your inner body and increase your sexual ability, if they are correctly practiced every day.

I have received many letters from men around the world thanking me for teaching these exercises, as they are very happy with the results. I even heard from some in their late sixties who wrote to say that problems such as impotence and premature ejaculation no longer existed.

Exercises:

1. Eagle Grasping

This first exercise should be practiced as many times a day as possible and can be done sitting, standing, lying down or even walking. Doing this will increase the supply of blood to the penis which will keep the erection stronger and help prevent premature ejaculation.

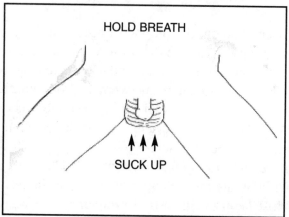

HOLD BREATH

SUCK UP

-Inhale and suck up both your testicles and your anus as hard as you can while holding your breath as long as you can.

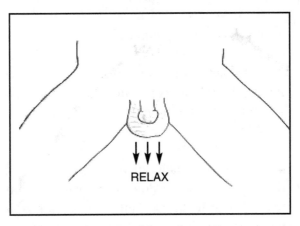

RELAX

-<u>Exhale</u> as you let your testicles and anus relax

It is a good idea in the beginning to stand in front of a mirror while doing this exercise so you can see your testicles rise as you are sucking up and lowering as you exhale.

2. Gorilla Sitting

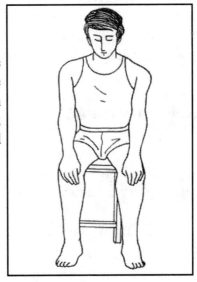

This exercise is very important for controlling ejaculation and the more you practice it, the more powerful the benefits, such as decreased impotence, decreased nervousness, and increased energy.

1. Sit up straight on the edge of a chair with your feet flat on the floor about shoulder width apart. You should wear loose pants or nothing at all, so your testicles can hang freely.

2. Relax your whole body.

3. Put your tongue at the roof of your mouth and inhale slowly through your nose filling your lungs, while at the same time slightly sucking up your testicles and anus.

4. Hold your breath, lower your body a little and then push all the air downward past your navel toward your testicles. Hold your breath as long as you can. Exhale and relax.

Repeat this exercise five times to make up a set. After one set stand up, move your hips, shake your legs and arms, then repeat the entire set again.

The prostate gland will be massaged by the tightening action of the PC and anus muscles. Take care to keep your shoulders and face relaxed. You will see great results if you do this every day for two months. If you do this exercise correctly, your body will get very warm and you should feel a tingling sensation in your testicles. Like any exercise, you only get out of it what you put into it.

3. Kidney Rub

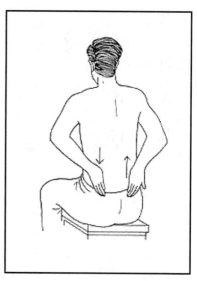

1. Rub your hands together to get them warm.

2. Inhale, hold your breath.

3. then bend over a little and rub your kidneys up and down 81 times.

4. Exhale.

This exercise should be done twice a day, once in the morning and once in the evening. You can do this sitting or standing.

4. Controlling Ejaculation

When I first began my lovemaking training with Master Hsu and Yo-Eko, I remember how difficult it was to control my ejaculation. In order to help me with this Master Hsu would sometimes stop what we were doing and have me lie on my back. Yo-Eko would then sit on top of me and move back and forth with my penis in her vagina. When I was getting close to ejaculation, he had Yo-Eko stop moving and had me pull my toes back hard while inhaling, suck up as hard as I could and hold my breath. When I couldn't hold it any longer I would exhale slowly through my nose, not releasing the tension in my toes or anus muscles. Master Hsu had us do this technique several times over and over again.

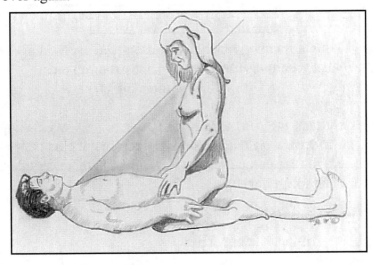

This exercise requires the help and understanding of your mate, but afterwards, the rewards will surely be worth the practice.

5. Sensitivity Exercise

For many men the head of the penis is overly sensitive. This can cause them to ejaculate prematurely. This simple exercise can help desensitize the head of the penis and will make it possible to better control ejaculation.

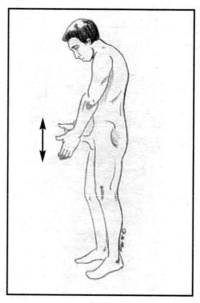

In a standing or sitting position take the head of the penis between the palms of your hands and rub them firmly back and forth for about three minutes.

This will decrease sensitivity during lovemaking without decreasing the pleasure. If you are not circumcised be sure to first pull back your foreskin. Do this every day, once or twice a day.

6. Stopping Ejaculation

Another way to help control ejaculation is by using the "pressing" technique. It can be used in almost any position without interrupting the lovemaking because the man applies the pressure to himself.

The Taoists believe that by pressing the Huei-Yin

point, located on the man's perineum between the anus and scrotum that ejaculation can be reversed, and that the semen will be recycled into the blood. After ejaculating, a man often loses interest and feels tired or lacks energy. But by applying pressure to the Huei-Yin point, he will remain energetic and have dramatically increased his ability to maintain his erection.

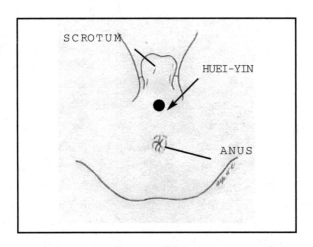

When you feel that orgasm is near, take your middle finger and press the Huei-Yin point. Do not press too hard or too softly. Breath deeply into your abdomen and hold it. Suck up your pelvic floor muscles, tightening your anus muscle as hard as you can. The semen will naturally stop. You will feel a throbbing sensation and soon your erection will go partially down. Keep pressing, then after the throbbing has stopped and you have control of yourself, intercourse may resume. Your erection will return and will be as strong or stronger than before.

Please Note: If you suffer from any prostate disorder, you should not do this exercise until you have consulted with your doctor.

According to Taoist wisdom, if you massage the Huei-Yin point every day it will help prevent any prostrate problem.

6. Urination Exercise

It was in November 1979 while I was in Taiwan that Master Hsu explained how people should practice strengthening their bodies as many times a day as possible, and that even urination could be used as an opportunity to do this.

I remembered how funny it looked when he demonstrated how an old man went to the bathroom. He pretended to pull out his penis and stand there trying to urinate; he makes faces and moves his hips a little, then, a little dribble. He tips his hip forward again, hoping it will start flowing, and again, a little dribble. He twitches again, then a sigh of relief; it's flowing! Then of course, he shakes it vigorously making sure all the urine is out. Funny as it was, it is the truth. He then demonstrated how a young boy went to the bathroom and how much faster he could go than the old man. He goes in, quickly pulls out his penis, and a starts a powerful flow of urine. With precision, he cuts off the flow, tucks his penis inside his pants and struts out.

Master Hsu felt there was no reason why there should be a difference in strength of urination between men and boys if men kept their inner organs strong.

The strength of urine flow is an important and easy way to determine one's sex power. If the flow is very forceful, then one's sexual power is rather great; but if it is very weak and even dribbling, one's sexual power is in decline. In order to test this theory, you can observe your own urination to see which is more forceful; discharge just before sexual intercourse or discharge when you are sick. It is usually stronger during sexual arousal and weaker if the body is ill. The Taoists say also that a man should not urinate right after intercourse as some of the sexual energy that is still in his body will be urinated out.

This exercise is very simple and natural:

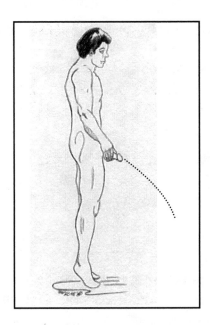

When you go to urinate, stand up on your toes as high as you can and keep your back straight. Lock the buttocks and forcibly discharge the urine while slowly exhaling. Practice cutting it off mid-stream.

Caution: Do not do this exercise every time you urinate as there is a risk of infection if a small amount of urine is habitually retained.

8. Hip Rotation Exercise

This exercise will help to strengthen the kidneys, relieve back pain, release tension and improve digestion. Especially in men, the sacrum and the hips can eventually become fused if not exercised. In the beginning this exercise may be difficult to do, but after a while you will be able to separate the hips from the sacrum and move more freely. This will also enable chi to travel up the Governor channel more easily. Because many men have restricted movement in this area, they tend to use only simple thrusts during love-making which stimulates just a small part of the vagina. By being able to rotate the hips while thrusting, the entire vagina will be stimulated and great pleasure will be given to your lover.

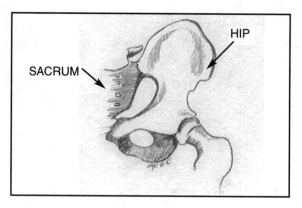

Put your hands on your hips and rotate or circle your hips. Do this at least 50 times to the right, and 50 times to the left.

Recommended Frequency for Ejaculation

Men cannot expect to refrain from ejaculation all the time, but frequency of ejaculation should be in line with age and season. The Taoists believe that ejaculation should be controlled and that a man should have control of his penis, not be controlled by his penis. A man need not ejaculate every time he makes love. This is especially true if he is fifty years old or older. If a man can accept this advice, he is potentially a more effective sexual partner.

Whether a man is young, old, weak or strong if he seeks only the pleasure of ejaculation, his health will be damaged. The Taoists believe these rules of ejaculation should be followed:

A healthy male of twenty years can ejaculate once in four days, or if he is weak then only once in eight days.

A healthy male of thirty years can ejaculate once in eight days, or if he is weak then only once every 16 days.

46

A flourishing male of forty years can ejaculate once every 16 days, or if he is weak once in 30 days.

A vigorous man of fifty can ejaculate once in 21 days, and only once every 2 months if he is weak.

A vigorous man of sixty can ejaculate once a month, or if he is weak then he should avoid it altogether.

A vigorous man of seventy years can ejaculate once every sixty days, or better yet only once every ninety days.

The Taoists believe that having sex at 100 is very healthy, however it is best not to ejaculate at all.

Men of any age should engage in intercourse as often as possible, the more the better. However, frequency of ejaculation should also be in harmony with the seasons. During winter a man should refrain from ejaculation as much as possible due to the fact that this is the season when all of nature goes dormant. Animals hibernate, trees lose their leaves, and the level of chi in the body is generally lower than during the warmer seasons. As spring moves into summer, more frequent ejaculation will not exact such a toll on a man's body as the level of chi is generally higher. This is the way of nature. If this rule can be obeyed, one will enjoy good health and a long life. The Taoists believe that one ejaculation in winter is equivalent to at least ten ejaculations in summer or spring.

Chapter 4

INCREASING STRENGTH AND
POWER IN WOMEN

Tightening Vaginal Muscles

It was Master Chiao who taught me how important it was for women to learn how to strengthen their vaginal muscles. One day he had me come to his office where a young woman was waiting. He was going to teach the Shih-Shui exercises for women. At his request she took off her clothes and sat on the floor. She had only been doing the first exercise for a few minutes when she began to perspire heavily. It wasn't an external exercise that made her perspire, but the internal work of special breathing and tightening of the vaginal muscles. I observed Master Chiao teaching this woman as well as others every day for three weeks so that I could also learn to teach women Shih-Shui and other chi kung exercises.

With regular practice these exercises can eventually stop menstruation. The inner organs are triggered to redirect the flow of blood, which would otherwise be lost, to nourish and strengthen the sexual glands and other internal organs. As this happens quite naturally during pregnancy, nursing and menopause, and no drugs are involved, there is no need for concern that this may be an unnatural thing to do. These exercises can also eliminate many problems related to the menstrual cycle such as emotional ups and downs, water retention, cramps, hormone blockages, and irregular flow of blood.

Please note: Do not do these exercises if you are pregnant.

The following exercises will strengthen and tighten the vaginal muscles, which can greatly enhance sexual pleasure for both partners. They will also have the effect of packing chi into the ovaries and vagina making arousal and orgasm easier and will also increase estrogen levels which can greatly relieve the symptoms of menopause and rejuvenate a woman. If practiced correctly and regularly, these exercises will make a woman's vagina very tight even if she has given birth to numerous children.

1. Eagle Grasping

This exercise can be done almost any time, anywhere; while walking, lying down, sitting at your desk in the office or driving your car. The beauty of it is that no one will know you are doing it!

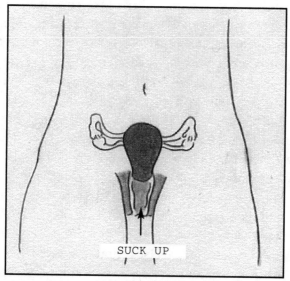

SUCK UP

Inhale as you suck up both your vaginal and your anus muscles as hard as you can. At the same time, hold your breath as long as you can.

50

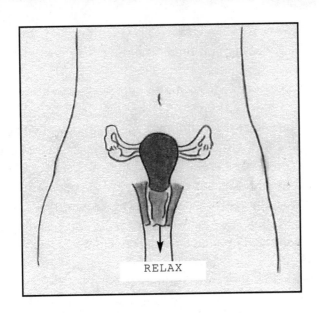

Relax as you exhale.

In the beginning, it is a good idea to put a mirror between your legs so you can actually see how your vagina contracts. This will help you to better visualize the contractions as you do this exercise.

2. Phoenix Perching on a Tree

This is a very good exercise. Do this first thing in the morning and right before going to bed at night.

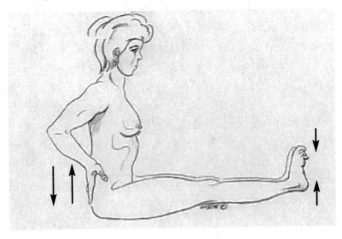

-Sit on a firm mattress or on the floor with your back straight and your legs straight out in front of you.

- Put your tongue on the roof of the mouth.

- Inhale slowly through your nose down into your pelvis. At the same time push your heels forward so

that they rise up off the floor, pull your toes back hard and curl them down. Hold your breath.
- Tighten your anus and vaginal muscles as hard as you can, compressing the air.

- Hold your breath as long as you can while rubbing your hands up and down on the kidneys and many times as you can.

- Exhale slowly through your nose and relax your body and toes.

Repeat the entire exercise at least three times. If you are doing it correctly your body will become very warm. The more you can do this exercise, the greater and swifter the results will be.

3. Urination Exercise

When Master Hsu demonstrated how men should strengthen their bodies at every opportunity, even during urination, he said the same applied to women. He gave a similar demonstration, pretending to be an old woman going to the bathroom. She stresses and grimaces, then; a little dribble! She tries a few more times until she is able to empty her bladder completely. A young girl on the other hand will go to the bathroom and get right down to business and be at the sink freshening up much faster than an older woman. But, Master Hsu again felt there was no reason why there should be a difference in strength of urination between girls and women if women kept their inner organs strong.

This exercise is very simple and natural:

Stand on your toes and do not touch the toilet seat with your buttocks. Force the urine out and practice cutting it off mid-stream.

Caution: Do not do this every time you urinate as there is a risk of infection if a small amount of urine is habitually retained.

Using this technique will build up energy in the kidneys. A decline in kidney energy usually results in weak kidneys, general fatigue, bladder problems, incontinence, and diminished sexual power.

4. Hip Rotation Exercise

This exercise will help to strengthen the kidneys and ovaries, relieve back pain, release tension, and improve digestion. The sacrum and hips can eventually become fused if they are not exercised. In the beginning this exercise may be difficult to do, but after a while you will be able to separate the hips from the sacrum and move more freely. This will also facilitate the flow of chi up the Governor channel.

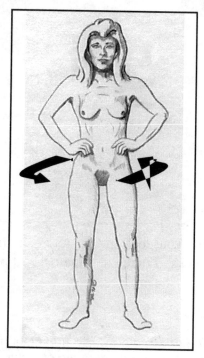

Put your hands on your hips and rotate or circle your hips. Do this at least 50 times to the right, then 50 times to the left.

Chapter 5

FOREPLAY, KISSING & LICKING

At the beginning of my training with Yo-Eko, Master Hsu talked to me about foreplay and how important it was not to skip or minimize this stage of lovemaking. He talked about the different ways to touch, hold and kiss a woman and how it all should be done with beauty and feeling. He had me look into her eyes and then slowly and tenderly kiss her lips, her chin, her cheek, ear, nose and forehead. At the same time he said, I should run my hands softly over her hair and down her back and arms. I gently caressed all parts of her body, hips and legs while deliberately avoiding her breasts and vagina. I practiced this over and over again with Master Hsu directing and advising me and Yo-Eko telling me what she felt and how I could make it better. After a couple of hours of this I would get so excited I found it very difficult to refrain from ejaculation. Master Hsu reminded me that my training would not be easy. Finally, after kissing, caressing and feeling her body for what seemed like days I was allowed to slowly unbutton her blouse and slide off her skirt. I was going crazy. I had to be inside her! Master Hsu told me to concentrate on what I was doing, but I was very aroused. My penis was very hard and it was difficult to concentrate. "Get your mind out of your pants!" he yelled.

We practiced this "heaven and hell" foreplay many times. Heaven because I was kissing and caressing this gorgeous, almost naked young woman and hell because I wanted more than anything the one thing I was forbidden to

55

have with her: sex.

When we finally went home for dinner I could hardly walk because my testicles hurt so much. (You may know this condition as "Blue Balls," a common and painful occurrence for men who have been aroused but have not ejaculated.) It had been a very long day and I was glad it was over, but it also felt good knowing that I somehow had done the impossible. I had made it through that day without ejaculating.

A few nights later, after kung-fu class was over and all the students had left, Master Hsu told me some more things about kissing and foreplay. He said, "The Taoists believe that the woman should always be completely and fully satisfied through intercourse. This is why foreplay is so very important. With the right kind and duration of foreplay her vagina will become lubricated and her mind and body will become ready for intercourse.

The ultimate objective of foreplay between a man and a woman is to attain the harmony of Yin and Yang before intercourse begins. Woman strives to make man hard and man strives to make woman soft. Couples must become attuned to each other in order to achieve a balanced and harmonious sexual act. A man must be kind and loving and a woman must be enduring and determined."

In Taoist lovemaking there should not be any inhibitions or areas of the body that can not be touched or caressed. If both partners are relaxed and communicating well, they will be able to respond correctly to each other's needs and wants. Foreplay must be approached with an open and frank attitude. Although there are no time limits or set patterns of action, foreplay is definitely more than a kiss on the lips and the squeeze of a breast.

It is recommended to begin with sensitive touching, not at the genitals, but at the body's extremities. A simple, sincere touch or caress on a hand or face can elicit a feeling of love speeding throughout the body. This also allows sexual energy to accumulate and grow in the genitals. Allow yourself to really feel your partner's body with all your attention. Touch can let your partner know that at this moment no one else matters.

One of the most neglected aspects of foreplay is kissing. Such a simple act, yet it is usually done only briefly or unimaginatively during the initial stages of fore-play. To the Taoists, erotic kissing and licking are invalu-able techniques to be taken very seriously during lovemaking. Among the infinite variety of possible kisses, great pleasure can be derived from long sensual kisses while light feathery kisses all over the body can create sen-sations never before felt.

One evening, Master Hsu made a point of stating that the Taoist way of loving must be accepted before it can be mastered, and that if I could not accept this then I should not continue. I told him, "But, I do accept the Taoist ways." I did not realize how little I knew. I knew nothing of kiss-ing for example, but was soon to find out.

In October, 1980 I was in Taiwan with Mei-Tsu and her girlfriend, May-Hwa. I thought by then I was a very good kisser and lover as it was my second year learning the art of lovemaking. As I mentioned earlier, I was kissing Mei-Tsu when May-Hwa interrupted us and asked me to kiss her. I noticed she was kissing differently. I had never felt anything like this before, but by the time I tried to imi-tate her it was too late! She abruptly stopped and told Master Hsu, "He is kissing wrong. He is kissing like a man kisses a woman, not like a woman kisses a woman." I did-n't know there was a difference.

Master Hsu asked the two women to demonstrate. I became very aroused as I watched Mei-Hwa kiss Mei-Tsu. It was so beautiful; so sensuous and loving. Her lips just barely touching Mei-Tsu's as they glided with a softness lighter than that of a feather. As their extended tongues met and played, the vibration of energy flowing between them was almost tangible. It was obvious to me that they were taking great pleasure and delight in what they were doing.

I practiced with each of them again and found they each kissed very differently. This time I tried to let my lips be very soft and I focused on remaining completely aware as I tried to kiss with as much sensitivity and feeling as I could. Over time kissing became a very different experi-ence for me.

During one of our lessons Master Hsu stated that there are three places on the body that must be kissed in order to harmonize Yin and Yang of the body and to gain the benefit of its fluids.

The first is the mouth. The exchange of saliva that takes place during kissing in beneficial to both partners. The saliva will change in quality according to arousal. I remembered kissing Yo-Eko and how much I savored her kisses. Kissing her was like sipping the dew from a flower petal. The Taoists feel that deep erotic kissing is as good as actual intercourse. Oral or genital kissing is regarded as a very effective way of arousing a man or a woman. Kissing deeply and often will keep both partners aroused during lovemaking.

The second is the breasts. The fluid that comes from the woman's nipples is clear and sweet to the taste. Drinking this will strengthen her blood circulation and relax her body. During one of my sessions with Yo-Eko, Master Hsu showed me how to caress her breasts by swirling over them with the palms of my hands, using the slightest touch. Then came the squeezing of the nipple, gentle but firm, while circling it with the tip of my tongue - moving it sideways as a change of pace then slowly sucking her breast like a baby drinking milk from his mother. This is usually a very enjoyable and arousing experience for a woman if it is done with sensitivity. But not all women's nipples are pleasantly sensitive to this type of stimulation. However, if she gently persists, she may learn to love this.

The third is kissing the vagina. Most women love this and a man should take his time and enjoy it as much she does. Move your tongue different ways and relax your mouth. Listen and feel for her needs and wants and do not stop until she has an orgasm.

Every part of the body can be kissed and licked from head to toes. Sensitive erotic kissing can in itself be very gratifying and even if you are too tired to really make love, you can still enjoy lovingly holding and kissing each other.

It had been about a week since Yo-Eko and I had practiced "heaven and hell" when Master Hsu arranged for me to meet her again. This time he would teach me how to make love to her with my penis, but only if the foreplay was done correctly. We started as slowly as we did before. After about an hour and a half of caressing, slowly undressing and fondling each other, we took a break. I sure needed it and I know Yo-Eko was very aroused too. She went into the bathroom and was in there for quite a while, and when Master Hsu yelled at her to come out she came out with a smile.

Yo-Eko got dressed and we started again. Master Hsu said that this time I could slowly take off her bra and panties. She told Master Hsu she did not know if she could stand it much longer as she was very excited and still wet. He smiled and said he would not stop me again, IF I did everything right. He assured her that she would be satisfied so we started over again from the beginning.

The soft kissing soon turned into passion. I started to lose it and before I knew it I was going straight for her vagina. Master Hsu yelled, "Slow down, take your time, feel her body's emotions, don't go there yet!" We both were very turned on, but I slowed down, and continued feeling, caressing and loving every inch of her body. She went wild, touching herself, and arching her back. I began licking her breasts the way I was taught, and slowly inching my hand down to her lovely vagina. Finally I felt the sweet lips of her vagina. She was soaked. I had never felt a vagina as wet!

She looked down at me and whispered sweetly, "Kiss me." But before I could, Master Hsu yelled out, "Not yet, feel it like I taught you." I felt her clitoris, it was as hard as my penis so I slowly inserted my finger in her vagina. Yo-Eko cried out in ecstasy when I started rubbing her G-spot and running my tongue across her clitoris. I kept my tongue on her vagina as she bucked like a wild horse. She fell to the bed exhausted, but smiling. Master Hsu said, "Now hold her softly and don't try to play with her, just hold her with feeling." He walked out of the room and Yo-Eko rested in my arms. She turned and gave me a kiss and said "Thank-you". I looked at her. She was so beautiful. I said, "No, thank you".

When Master Hsu returned he said, "Let's get up and

take a break. Later I will teach you how to really love her, but this time with your penis."

When Yo-Eko went into the bathroom Master Hsu explained to me, "Do not insert your fingers or penis into her vagina until you are sure she is at her highest emotional peak and thoroughly lubricated. Only when you observe the "Five Signs of Desire" (see page 70), should you proceed further. There are three things you must remember: First, learn the recommended frequency of ejaculation to suit your age and state of health. This will allow you to make love whenever you or your partner wish and continue making love for as long as it takes for your partner to reach complete satisfaction.

Second, remember that uncontrolled ejaculation is not the ultimate pleasure. Once you understand this, you can enjoy much more fulfillment during lovemaking. This will also make it easier for you to control your ejaculation.

The third and most important point is that you must fully satisfy the woman. Women are easily and too often left unsatisfied. Be sure that you are doing all that you can to allow for good communication so that you will know how to satisfy her. Always take the time to just hold her so that you can really feel her emotions.

These three things are basic to the Taoist way of making love and will lead you to experience the infinite harmony of yin and yang."

Chapter 6

MALE SATISFACTION

In general, men enjoy many of the same physical pleasures that women do. They too like to be kissed and caressed and massaged with loving care. Playful teasing can be as much fun and arousing for a man as it is for a woman and sometimes the simple pleasure of being lovingly held in her arms can be the most satisfying. In addition to the attention and physical stimulation a woman can offer her man, the more fully she can accept and enjoy his loving toward her, the more pleased and gratified he will be.

During the days I spent in the house on the mountain I had many conversations with Yu-Lin about sexual matters. She discussed with me some of the things a woman must know before she can fully please her man. She stressed the great importance of clear and uninhibited communication as well as cleanliness. One of the most important things both men and women can do before making love, is to be sure that they are clean. Traces of urine or other secretions can quickly make their bodies smell very bad and unappetising. It is wise for both to take a shower or bath as part of their foreplay.

When making love to a man, a woman must relax and learn to feel with all her senses his reactions and desires as she lovingly touches, holds and caresses him. She must communicate freely with him, asking him if he is enjoying her touch and tell him how much she is enjoying the pleasures of loving him. This type of verbal communication does not come easily to many women, but with a little practice it will soon become more comfortable. The effort will almost certainly be very appreciated and will open the way to a richer more intimate lovemaking experience. Yu-Lin said if a woman is very attentive she can know what her partner desires from her. If he holds her tightly, most likely he too wants to be held tightly; if he is kissing her softly, she will know that he would like to be kissed softly, and so on.

A wonderful way for a woman to give a man great pleasure is to make love to his penis with her mouth. However, doing it is one thing, but doing it with pleasure is quite another and a man will definitely be able to tell the difference. If the woman is enjoying it, then he will enjoy it even more.

The first thing she must learn before making love to a man's penis is to relax her throat muscles. In most cases a penis is larger than a woman's throat, but if she can relax enough she can overcome the gagging that automatically happens when something goes into the throat. This gag reflex is nature's way of closing off the throat and pushing out whatever is in it in order to prevent choking. To overcome a natural reflex such as this can be quite tricky at first. It is very important that the man not become impatient and force his penis deeper into his partner's mouth before she is quite ready as this will cause her great discomfort and pain during a moment that should be very loving and intimate."

Yu-Lin said that I must first learn how to relax my own throat before I could teach my students how to do it. She had me put one finger into my throat and when nothing happened, she told me to go deeper. I of course gagged and automatically pulled out my finger, coughing and clutching my throat. She laughed and said, "You need a lot of practice! Remember, you can't teach it if you can't do it yourself." She had me try it a few more times until I could do it without gagging.

"Now", she said, "Put two fingers into your throat." I did and began to gag even more than before. Yu-Lin kept repeating, "Relax, relax, relax. Now put one finger into your throat and when the gagging sensation begins hold

62

your finger there and try to relax your throat even more."
Over and over we tried until I gained control over this
reflex. At that point Yu-Lin smiled at me and said,
"Congratulations, you have just passed the first stage!"

She turned around and pulled out a small crystal
dildo. She said, "Pretend for a moment that you are a
woman and I am a man. This is my penis and I want you to
suck it now." She put the dildo into my mouth and forced it
down my throat so hard that tears came to my eyes. I panicked and couldn't breathe, and wondered at the same time
why she would suddenly be so cruel and insensitive. She
pulled it out and with a little laugh she said, "Now you
know what you must never do to a woman. Too many
women have had to endure this kind of pain from their
lovers. By the time you complete your training you are
going to appreciate a good 'cock sucker'. "With one hand
holding my throat and the other wiping the tears from my
eyes I managed to laugh too and said, "I already do!"

Next, she told me to lie on my back with my head
bent over the edge of the bed. "This will open up your
throat and make it easier for you to relax your muscles," she
explained. She slowly inserted the dildo again into my
throat and told me that when I felt the gagging sensation
begin, I should tap her on the leg. Needless to say I was a
little more nervous now and no sooner had she put it in than
I was tapping her on the leg. She pulled it out a little and
when she saw me relax, slowly pushed it in again. She left
it there for a moment and then slowly pushed it in a little
deeper. My heart started to pound and I felt like I was going
to choke and tapped her leg again. She then pulled it back
just a little and told me to breath deeply into my abdomen
and relax my throat muscles. We practiced this until I
seemed to have gotten the knack of it.

If a man wishes to get the full benefit of this type of
oral sex he must understand and be very sensitive to what
the woman is going through in order to please him.

Yu-Lin then strapped the dildo on to her body as if
she were the man and laid down on her back with her
"penis" sticking straight up. She then instructed me to get
on top of her and go down on her. I put the dildo into my

mouth and tried to devour it. I found that in this position I was easily able to control its depth and could pull back whenever I felt any discomfort or gagging.

Yu-Lin re-emphasized how important it was to make it as easy as possible for the woman to enjoy the pleasure of sucking her man's penis. Too often a man will simply shove his penis deep into the woman's throat not seeming to care that it hurts her because all he is interested in is ejaculating. He must be loving and sensitive. Yes, in time she can learn how to put a penis deep into her throat, but the emotional and physical pain of being forced takes away all the pleasure for her.

Yu-Lin sat up and instructed me further on how to make love to her strapped on penis. She said, "You should start by slowly licking the head of the penis while holding it firmly at the base with your fingers. Work your tongue around and over the head and then start to move your lips up and down the hard shaft. At first let your lips and fingers be soft, and then try applying firmer pressure. Use a variety of ways of licking, kissing, sucking, caressing, holding, squeezing and stroking until you are sure your partner is happy. Most of all, enjoy what you are doing."

During my next session with Yu-Lin, she invited Ting-Ting to join us. She turned to me and said, "Now that you know how to 'suck a cock' I am going to instruct Ting-Ting in the art of satisfying a man, as if she were just learning, so that you may more fully understand how to teach women." She motioned me to the bed and had me sit there and wait. I knew this was going to be great.

When Ting-Ting was ready she came in and sat down beside me. Yu-Lin told Ting-Ting to begin by kissing me on the lips, softly and tenderly. She rubbed her fingers through my hair and on my neck and back. Yu-Lin said, "Now, look into his eyes and tell him how much you enjoy making love to him. Tell him how good he feels and how much you enjoy being with him."

Ting-Ting smoothed her hand over my chest and began caressing my nipples. Yu-Lin commented that, "Some men's nipples are very sensitive, but other men do not get excited from this sort of stimulation. A woman must feel his reaction to her touch and if she finds that this does not arouse him she should not spend much time in that area. You can tell by the way he moves or by the sounds he makes if he is interested in having this done or not. I can tell you that Jim does not get excited when someone plays with his nipples." This was true!

Ting-Ting continued to caress my body, running her soft hands all over my back, my hips and my stomach, slowly working her way down toward my rising penis. Yu-Lin then had her rub her hand lightly over my by now very swollen penis. She said, "As you can tell, the harder it gets the more sensitive his penis is." Ting-Ting had so much feeling in her hands; she seemed to really enjoy what she was doing. We slowly began to remove each other's clothing.

Ting-Ting lowered her mouth onto my now very hard penis. I noticed there was already some fluid glistening on the tip of it. She began licking the head of it with the tip of her tongue using a swirling motion while caressing my testicles with her other hand. It felt so good! Then she used her fingers to stroke up and down and then hold the shaft of my penis as she began sucking on the head of it. Yu-Lin had Ting-Ting stop at that point, explaining to her that she was "cheating." She told Ting-Ting, "Making love to a man's penis is an art, not a test of endurance. You were using more hand stroking than anything else. Unless he perfers otherwise, use your mouth as much as possible. This is one of the most pleasurable things a woman can do for a man and if done correctly she can receive much pleasure from it too."

Yu-Lin had her begin again saying, "This time, tighten your lips as firmly as you can around his penis and be very careful not to use your teeth. As you stroke up and down try to breathe normally through your nose. If you hold your breath you will lose your timing and concentration and will most likely start to choke. Use your mouth to rhythmically stroke up and down on his penis." I was definitely enjoying this. It was delightful to watch her devour my penis with so much pleasure. Yu-Lin further explained to Ting-Ting, "Looking into a man's eyes will get him even more excited and cause his penis to get harder. Eye contact is very important. You will know if he is enjoying what you are doing and if it is giving him satisfaction.

Now Jim will not be ejaculating, but when you are with your boyfriend and you feel that his ejaculation is close, go up and down his shaft and take his ejaculate in your mouth, not in your throat as this may cause you to choke. Semen is the purest, most highly energized and nutritious substance produced in a man's body. It is this, after all, in conjunction with the woman's egg that will pro-duce new life. So go ahead and swallow it and enjoy its healthful benefits. Consider it a precious gift from the man you love."

Yu-Lin turn to me then and said. "After ejaculating in a woman's mouth, the man should kiss her so that they may share in the exquisite essence of the moment together."

Chapter 7

FEMALE SATISFACTION

Clitoris and G-Spot

Knowing how to satisfy a woman is the third essential component of Taoist lovemaking. Women have many areas of their bodies that can be stimulated to increase their desire, not the least of which are the clitoris and the G-spot.

The clitoris is very sensitive and like the penis, it has a spongy portion that fills with blood and causes it to become erect when aroused. The clitoris can expand to about one inch when fully aroused, allowing for closer contact with the man's body. It is usually about 3/4 inch long, but only the tip projects while the body of it is hidden.

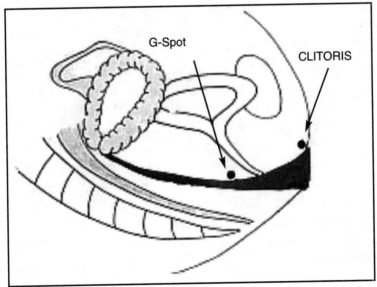

The G-spot is another area of high sensitivity and a potential source of great pleasure for a woman. The G-spot can be explored by feeling around the front and upper part of the inside of the vagina. It is about the size of a quarter and feels rougher in texture than the rest of the vagina which is very smooth. During sexual excitement these blood vessels engorge and a bulge can be felt through the vaginal wall. When her G-spot is first stimulated, a woman may have the urge to urinate, but if she allows the pressure to build, she will become very aroused and have a great orgasm.

The G-spot can be difficult to reach during intercourse in the face to face position, therefore couples should experiment with different angles of penetration. A change in position may be necessary if a woman wants her G-spot stimulated more directly. Rear entry is one way, and fingers are often effective. If the woman is on top during intercourse she can position herself for optimal stimulation of this area. When the G-spot is stimulated to the point of orgasm, it will produce a fluid much like seminal fluid.

Female Ejaculation and Orgasm

Only if a woman is completely relaxed will she have a true orgasm. A woman's orgasm is completely different from that of a man's. Where he experiences a relatively sudden drop in desire, energy and sexual feeling, a woman experiences this in a slower more gradual way. The secretion a woman produces during orgasm is also not like that of a man. It has no odor or color and little nutritional value.

The Taoists discovered that a woman, when reaching the highest point of orgasm, is ejaculating (yes, ejaculating!) and will emit a clear fluid. Many women who have experienced this say that they were dismayed and embarrassed, feeling certain that they had urinated. Sad to say, they then learned to withhold this reaction and never did it again. Many people today have not even heard of or do not understand female ejaculation.

The fluid is clear and made up of about 75 percent water mixed with secretions from the Skene's gland from which it will spurt out like a geyser. While women can ejaculate cupfuls over hours, the average man spurts out a mere teaspoonful of semen in seconds. It is wonderful for a woman to have an orgasm, but it goes to another level if she has an ejaculation, and yet another if she has a climax which consists of both.

It was with one of the four girls, Su-ling, at the mountain house during my last week of training with Master Hsu that I first encountered this. Su-Ling was an expert in female orgasm and ejaculations. She said, "Making a woman have an orgasm is necessary, making her have an ejaculation is an added bonus, but bringing her both is the ultimate."

I was very curious about this when she invited me to make love with her. I held her and slowly starting kissing her lips and touching her. I traced my fingers and hands over her naked body all the time feeling for her wants and desires. After thirty to forty-five minutes of foreplay, I began to kiss and love her elegant vagina with my tongue and fingers until the wetness flowed from her. I slowly inserted my finger, raising it to her G spot. Her body writhed with intense pleasure and then she sighed and relaxed as she orgasmed. We then lay there, just holding each other and she said, "That was good, I needed that!"

After resting a while, we started up again. Su-Ling explained, "To intensify the feeling and to find what is called the true "Nectar of the Goddess," is to have what some people call an ejaculation. This can be done in different ways, depending on the woman. I want you to start licking my clitoris and inside my vagina." I gladly followed her directions. After a while she said I was to insert my finger and rub her G-spot like I had done before. Then in a quiet, passionate tone, Su-Ling said, "That's good, now please don't stop rubbing my G-spot, and keep licking my clitoris.......don't stop. Now take your other hand and touch lightly on the outside of my body, just over the G-spot. You should be able to feel your other finger."

While my finger was inside her vagina, rubbing her

G-spot, my other hand was on the corresponding area of her lower abdomen. I could feel my other finger rubbing back and forth. It was almost like rubbing two fingers together. Then she said, "That's too hard, a little softer, there that's it, now just hold it there. Keep licking me and rubbing my G-spot from the inside and leave your hand there." She soon cried out, "O my God, don't stop!" Her body arched and trembled while the ejaculation flowed from her like a fountain. I continued to lick her vagina, as the sweet tasting nectar soaked my hand and the bed under us. I was surprised at the quanity but it smelled so fresh and sweet I knew that this was definitely not urine. This truly was the "Nectar of the Goddess." As Su-Ling collapsed she said, "Oh, thank you, now please hold me," and she fell into a blissful sleep.

After a little while, Su-Ling woke up and we talked more about how important it is for the woman to experience the Nectar of the Goddess and the deep feelings of bliss and fulfillment it brings her. She then proceeded to tell me of another way to help a woman reach a wonderful level of pleasure. She said that after I get her very excited and very lubricated, I should put one of my fingers in her vagina. She spoke quietly saying, " I want you to slowly move your finger a little in my vagina and then put another finger by my anus, just barely touching. As I get more excited my anus muscles will relax and open up a little, and your other finger will be able to ease in slowly." I was ready! Just hearing what I was going to do had me excited and knowing the pleasure it would give Su-Ling intensified the excitement. She made it very clear that I must first feel the muscles relax in her anus and by no means push too hard. The finger should ease in by itself.

We lay down and started kissing. I found that I enjoyed kissing her this time much more than the last time. I guess this was because we had become a team. As we kissed each other everywhere, I ran my finger down her spine and teased her in any way I could until she got very excited. Then finally, it was time to insert my finger a little way into her vagina with the other finger just touching her anus. I was still kissing her and moving my finger up and down in her vagina when all of a sudden I could feel her anus muscle relax, and sure enough my other finger eased in a little. She told me to go very slowly and really feel the muscles relax as I penetrated her. Before long both fingers were thrusting back and forth deeply inside her lovely body. She then told me to kiss her clitoris and with the other finger turn up and rub her G- spot. I did that for about ten minutes and felt like I could do it forever. Her body was perspiring and soon she tensed and let out a scream from somewhere very deep inside her. I tasted the sweet Nectar of the Goddess again.

Guaranteed Sexual Satisfaction for the Woman

After foreplay, when the woman's vagina is saturated with secretion, she will be ready to receive your penis. When you feel she is ready, slowly insert your penis only one inch inside her vagina. Thrust only to the depth of one inch inside her and vary the angles of thrusting. After a few minutes ask her if she wants another inch. If she is ready she will let you know. Slowly go in another inch, and continue to use different angles of thrusts. Remember, the penetration depth should now be only two inches.

Again ask her with a very loving voice if she wants another inch. Then insert another inch, changing the tempo and angles of thrusting with only three inches of your penis going inside her. This will excite her very much. Take your time, be very attentive to her reactions and adjust your timing accordingly. Continue inserting only one more inch at a time and thrusting, for at least four or five minutes each time, only the amount of inches that are inside her vagina. Then when you only have about two inches left, ask her if she wants all of you inside her. When she says yes, thrust your penis hard inside her and tell her now she has it all. Just hold it inside her and DO NOT MOVE until she has completed her orgasm. Then hold her tenderly and tell her how much you care about her and how good it feels being inside her.

71

After a short while her vagina and hips will start to move. This is a sign that she is now ready to have sexual intercourse again. Choose any one of the Ten Ways described later in this book and start again.

Mastering this technique was torture. When I learned this I was with Yo-Eko and tried hard to follow Master Hsu's instructions, slowly giving her only an inch of my penis at a time. However, it didn't take long before I was losing control and had to withdraw. I started over, but Master Hsu said, "You don't have to start at the beginning this time because she is still wet." Yo-Eko agreed. Master Hsu continued, "Now, insert your penis only one inch inside her vagina and move it up and down." The warmth of her lubricated vagina felt so good and I wanted badly to ejaculate, but I tried hard to concentrate on Master Hsu's instructions. He said to move side to side. I did it about two times before I had to pull out. I turned to Master Hsu and said, "I am sorry, but I just couldn't do it any longer without ejaculating." He looked at me sternly and said, "I am not the one you need to apologize to, it is Yo-Eko." I looked at her sheepishly but she just smiled and said that it was all right.

We tried again and again, inch by inch, over and over again. I kept pulling out and starting again. I thought the day would never end. I wondered how anyone could ever learn this. Many times I just wanted to say "Forget it, it's not worth it. I just want to ejaculate now." But I did not.

An hour or so went by and I started to notice that I did not have the same urge to ejaculate anymore. My semen must have been backed up so far inside me that I could not have even if I wanted to. I proceeded one inch at a time, as Master Hsu instructed, moving in and out, using different angles and speeds, each time moving in only an inch, until finally I had only about two inches left.

I asked her softly, "Do you want me to put it in all the way?" For the first time since we started I really noticed the glow on her face. Before I was thinking only of myself and her sweet, wet vagina, not even noticing how she looked. It was clear to me that she too wanted relief just as much as I did. I slid my penis in all the way, slowly, pushed hard and held it there. I didn't move. Her body arched and writhed under me and then lay still as the bliss of an intense orgasm washed through her.

Master Hsu said, "Hold her tenderly now and with feeling, don't withdraw your penis. I'll be back in a few minutes."

Yo-Eko fell asleep in my arms. She felt so good I thought I was in heaven. This time I was lying in the wet spot, but it was hers! I had not ejaculated and that made me feel very good also. A little later, Master Hsu walked in and said, "Get dressed and we will continue another day as you have much to learn. This is only the beginning."

The Five Signs of Female Desire

One evening prior to a session with Yo-Eko, Master Hsu explained that I must carefully observe the changes a woman goes through as she becomes aroused. As Yo-Eko and I proceeded to make love that night, he would stop me and ask if I had noticed changes in her skin color, temperature, breathing or behavior. The Taoists outlined the following typical signs of a women's desire :

1. Her face becomes warm and reddens. The excitement makes her breasts hard. This indicates she is becoming aroused and is enjoying the gentle touch of her lover. He should continue to tease and touch all over her body and be aware of her reactions.

2. She takes shorter breaths and begins to tremble. This indicates the fire of her lust is somewhat heightened. His penis can now go in to the depth of one or two inches but not much deeper than that. He should wait for her lust to further intensify before going in deeper.

3. Her throat becomes dry and coarse. She swallows her saliva and her voice is lowered. Her lust has intensified. Her eyes are closed and she pants audibly. At this time the man's penis should go in slowly another inch or

two, but no more, while continuing to move in and out freely with variations in movements.

4. Perspiration flows from her body. She is richly lubricated and the fire of her lust is nearing its peak. His thrusting method continues to change from left to right, slow and quick, up and down, so that each thrust causes the vaginal secretions to overflow. Now he may give her the full length of his penis.

5. Her body straightens and her eyes close as her fire and lust have now reached their peak. She wraps her legs around his waist and clutches his shoulders. As she reaches the ultimate, her mind goes empty, her desire fulfilled. The man should now hold her with tenderness and love as their bodies rest in harmony. After a short while she will be rested and then he should move in whatever way makes them both happy.

Master Hsu reminded me that a woman's level of arousal will rise and wane and that I must pay close attention to this. He went on to say that once the woman has reached orgasm it does not necessarily mean that it is time to stop making love but that I must feel and read her desire to know whether it is time to continue on to deeper levels of experience or to rest.

Stages of Arousal

For couples to fully enjoy their sexual potential, they must first have an understanding of the different levels of arousal and satisfaction that a woman will undergo. Master Hsu said, "You must study the different levels of female arousal. A woman having an orgasm can be described as a blooming flower. If she has a complete orgasm, she will undergo several stages of blossoming and only then will she open up and surrender herself to the man who has satisfied her." The Taoists have identified the following stages of female arousal:

1. She clasps the man in her arms and presses herself against him. While kissing him, she extends her tongue to arouse him.

2. She raises her knees from the bed desiring the outer parts of her genitalia to be touched and rubbed.

3. She arches her back and straightens her legs, desiring the feeling of his penis in her vagina.

4. She begins to move her buttocks more urgently, desiring more speed and force.

5. When she kicks or lifts her legs and grabs her feet, she is craving a deeper penetration.

6. When she twists her body to the right and left, she wants the thrusts to be slanted, so as to stimulate the sides of the vagina.

7. When she is perspiring and presses her vibrating body strongly against him, this indicates she does not want him to stop because her orgasm is near.

8. When she straightens her body and thrusts up so violently that he is pushed back, she is in the midst of an orgasm and is completely overcome by passion with no power of resistance.

9. When her body goes limp, her desire has been fulfilled.

10. When her vaginal fluids flow like running water, it means she has had an ejaculation or complete orgasm.

Once the woman reaches the fifth level, it becomes

easier for the man to bring her to higher levels of orgasm. Just a little movement can advance her to the next level, and beyond, until she reaches the tenth and final level of orgasm. The purpose of Taoist methods that prolong a man's erection is to give him the ability to advance a woman to this tenth level of orgasm.

Chapter 8

THE NINE STYLES OF THRUSTING

The Taoists devoted a great deal of time and study to the different angles, speeds and depths of thrusting. They realized that without a good understanding of these techniques, there could be little satisfaction for the woman. Taoist masters encouraged students to practice these variations and sometimes even recommended a certain number of thrusts for each position. Do keep in mind, however, that whatever the recommended number is, it is only a guideline, not a fast rule.

Master Hsu often referred to the Taoist saying "A thousand loving thrusts" as being the minimum amount required to genuinely satisfy a woman. At first I thought a thousand thrusts sounded more like hard work than sexual pleasure. I discovered, however, that the more I learned about and practiced the Taoist ways of loving, the more energy I had, the longer I lasted and the more I enjoyed it. A thousand thrusts was a thousand thrusts of pure rejuvenating pleasure. How could I ever get too much? It was also very gratifying to know I could give such pleasure and satisfaction to a woman. One thousand thrusts really only takes about fifteen minutes, and the effort is usually well rewarded. A fully satisfied woman will try harder to satisfy you because she will always remember the loving she has received from you.

When you have learned the Taoist way of lovemaking, you can easily make love for as long as you want. However, not all women are ready for two or three hours of lovemaking. Take care to hear and understand your partner so that you can be in harmony with her needs and wants.

Sometimes if you just want a "quickie" and if your partner feels the same way, it can be just as fulfilling. Even many highly sexed couples do not want prolonged love-making every day. But, it is important not to get in the habit of always doing quickies. Lovemaking is best done when you both have the time and are not tired. When that time comes you should love every inch of her body and experiment with variations of different techniques. But even if you are very tired, you can still take a moment to lovingly-hold each other.

The most important point to note here is that you will never again have to disappoint your partner or yourself once you have learned and accepted the Taoist way of love-making.

During intercourse, you must practice controlling the actions of your penis. Do not stab at a woman's vagina, but respond to her reactions. The following different styles of thrusting can be applied to any of the Ten Ways described in the next chapter. Experiment with all of them and adopt the styles that work best for both of you.

THE NINE STYLES:

1. A General Moving Through Battle Lines

The penis moves right and left with strong and deep penetrations, using only the pelvis to thrust.

When Master Hsu first watched me try this technique he started to laugh, saying I was too stiff and that I was moving too much of my body and wasting energy. He came around to the side of the bed and told me to watch how he moved his pelvis. He used a pencil as his penis and showed me how it should be done. I understood what he meant when I saw how little his body moved and yet the angle of the pencil varied greatly. I went back and tried again allowing my movements to be smaller and more subtle.

2. A Wild Horse Leaping over a Mountain River

The penis moves up and down deeply using strong and quick movements. This style is well suited for the position of "The Monkey Springs".

3. A Flock of Seagulls on the Waves

The penis moves down and then the pelvis tips upward as it draws back. The movement is rhythmical with deep and slow penetration and a quicker withdraw. The upward tipping of the pelvis is of great importance in providing mutual satisfaction between partners.

Master Hsu would help me understand this style by placing his hands on my hips and actually guiding my movements, showing how the pelvis should thrust down and then up as it draws back. The pelvis move in a bobbing rhythm similar to that of a seagull as it appears and disappears with the rise and fall of the ocean waves. He said this is the motion used in the nine shallow and one deep technique, after the nine shallows.

4. A Sparrow Pecking

The penis moves in recurrent deep and shallow penetrations. This includes the "nine shallow and one deep" pattern of penetration. By going shallow this allows for direct stimulation to the clitoris. This style is well suited to the position of "The Tortoise Mounts".

5. A Rock Tossed into the Ocean

Thrust from side to side and use only the movement of the pelvis. The penis initially penetrates shallow and soft, going deeper and deeper with each successive stroke, similar to a rock settling to the ocean floor.

Again, Master Hsu laughed when he saw me try this. "You are more like a brick," he said, "Think of the side to side motion a flat rock would make as it falls through the water and settles to the ocean floor." It looked so graceful and beautiful when he demonstrated it.

6. A Snake in Winter

The penis penetrates deeply and slowly and withdraws slowly with circling movements.

Here Master Hsu explained that snakes hibernate in the winter and if they move at all, it is with slow, purposeful, steady movements.

7. A Frightened Mouse Running Through a Hole

The penis penetrates quickly and withdraws quickly. The movements are strong and swift.

Master Hsu explained that this darting style is used by a rooster mating with a hen and also by many men. He demonstrated with his fingers how a rooster does it with a hen very fast, and then its all over. It looked very funny, but the sad thing is that many couples make love only this way. This is indeed a very good technique, but one of many. It should be done at the right time and with variations in the angle of thrust.

8. A Hawk Seizing its Prey

The penis moves in an erratic manner inside the woman's vagina. This style does not have any set patterns to its movement, and each thrust should be different than the preceding ones.

This style is almost like the Frightened Mouse

Running Through the Hole, except in this case a combination of all styles is used. Movements should be done in erratic manner and with self control.

9. A Sailboat in Strong Winds

The man gently teases the woman with the slow determined movement of his penis, thrusting up and down with restraint. This is a great beginning stroke during the initial stage of intercourse.

By practicing these various thrusts, you will be able to achieve true Taoist intercourse: intercourse that lasts much longer than the conventional one and is able to bring about a sensitivity and oneness never before experienced. Do not take the suggested numbers of thrusts, as in "nine shallow and one deep," too literally. These are only guidelines. If you sense that your partner would enjoy a longer interval or a variety of thrusts, then that is what you should do.

Chapter 9

THE TEN WAYS OF TAOIST LOVEMAKING

The Ten Ways or positions of intercourse consti-
tute an important aspect of Taoist lovemaking.
Sexual desire and sexual power are not easily controlled by
will and determination. Sometimes external stimulation is
needed in order for them to function properly. Erection of
the penis in the man, and orgasm in the woman, can take
place only through a variety of sensory stimulations involv-
ing sight, smell, taste, touch etc. The essential function of
the different positions is to supply such stimulation. Master
Hsu emphasized that intercourse should never be allowed to
become a routine affair. He explained, "Couples should not
only practice the Ten Ways, but should also use their imag-
inations to create new positions and styles that suit their
particular needs. However, before doing this it is important
to understand and accept the Taoist way of lovemaking.
The man must learn to control his ejaculation and understand the importance of fully satisfying the woman. Both
partners must become very sensitive to each other's emotions and desires and respond accordingly. They must
remember that their objective is to achieve the harmony of
yin and yang and ultimately, immortality. The energy generated during lovemaking must be allowed to accumulate
and then be circulated through their bodies in the Little
Nine Heaven Circle. In this way the 'ching' or sexual
essence can be transferred to the 'chi' or breath, which can

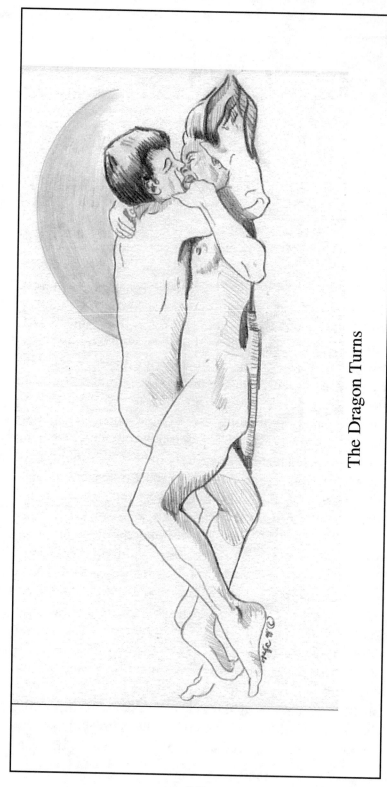

The Dragon Turns

then in turn be transferred to 'shen' or spirit. Shen must then be cultivated so that it may return to the state of 'shu' or emptiness. This is true Taoist lovemaking."

The first way is called **The Dragon Turns.** Master Hsu explained how it should be done: "Yo-Eko will lie down on her back, and you Jim, will lie on top of her, with your legs placed between her's. The woman may want to raise her buttocks with a pillow so that her vagina will be in closer touch with your penis, however, this depends on the woman and the angle of her vagina. Yo-Eko doesn't need it. Use your penis to vigorously stimulate her clitoris and then follow with slower movements of the penis, using the rhythm of **nine shallow and one deep.** The nine shallow penetrations create a vacuum inside the vagina which will delight her. The vacuum has tremendous effect. The one deep penetration gives a different sort of stimulation, forcing air out of her vagina. This should be a powerful but soft thrust. With this pattern of thrusts she will feel full, then empty, full, then empty; each deep penetration increasing her desire. Tip your pelvis up as you draw your penis back from each thrust, as this will cause it to rub more firmly across her G-spot. Then, circle the hips a few times as if the 'dragon' is turning. When Yo-Eko begins to feel these sensations, gradually she will become more excited until she reaches the point of orgasm. Once she has had a complete orgasm her vagina will naturally close and become firm. You must notice this."

This position is called "The Dragon Turns" because it refers to the turning of the penis like the flying of a dragon. It also refers to the man approaching the woman like a powerful dragon which gives him a sense of superiority and control over her. When you are on top, both your hands and feet are supporting your body giving you control over the amount of weight with which you bear down upon her. Your body weight gives her a sense of closeness, not only because of the feeling of being loved and overcome, but also because your weight is being placed on the two most sensual parts of her body, the breasts and the vagina, at the same time.

After the nine shallow one deep technique try dif-

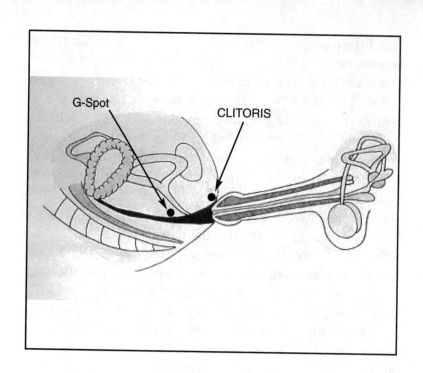

Nine Shallow

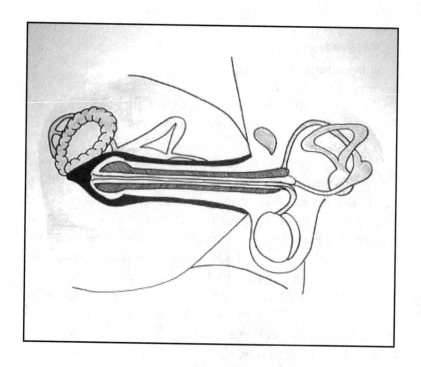

One Deep

ferent kinds of thrusting. Circle right and left, thrust fast, slow, long or short; use your imagination to vary your movements and create new combinations of thrusts and rhythms.

As I entered Yo-Eko I raised my body high enough to where I thought my penis was rubbing her clitoris. But Master Hsu told me to move up even higher. I did and silently counted my strokes. Nine shallow thrusts, then one deep thrust. Yo-Eko smiled, so I started again. Nine shallow thrusts, then, Oh no, not now! I was going to ejaculate! I had lost my concentration and started moving faster, losing control, and was rapidly approaching the point of no return. Master Hsu yelled, "Not yet, stupid!" and he slapped me hard on my rear, causing enough pain and humiliation to stop my on-coming ejaculation in its tracks. I pulled out and we took a break. Yo- Eko frowned, turned her back to me and just sat. Master Hsu was disgusted. "You must take your brain out of your penis and put it back in your head, do you understand?" I said, "Yes, sir." But what I really meant was, "How?" Master Hsu said we would stay all day and night if we had to until I could do it right. It was almost more than I could handle. We tried over and over again, but each time I had to pull out, either on the shallow thrusts or on the deep penetration. We had been there several hours before I finally managed to do it right. Yo-Eko was happy, Master Hsu was happy and I was happy just to go home - it had been a very long day.

The following Thursday after lunch, Master Hsu let me know we were going to see Yo- Eko that day and that I must do my best to maintain control. "Try to relax. Forget what you are doing and enjoy it," he said. When we met Yo-Eko it seemed like she wasn't really interested in being there. The feeling was different. I felt confused and blamed myself thinking, "Are we using her? I love her. I want to be with her forever!"

Master Hsu interrupted my thoughts by saying, "We are now going to do the next position. It is called **The Tiger Is Stalking**. This time the foreplay will only be about thirty minutes. In this position the man resembles a tiger ready to pounce on his prey.

87

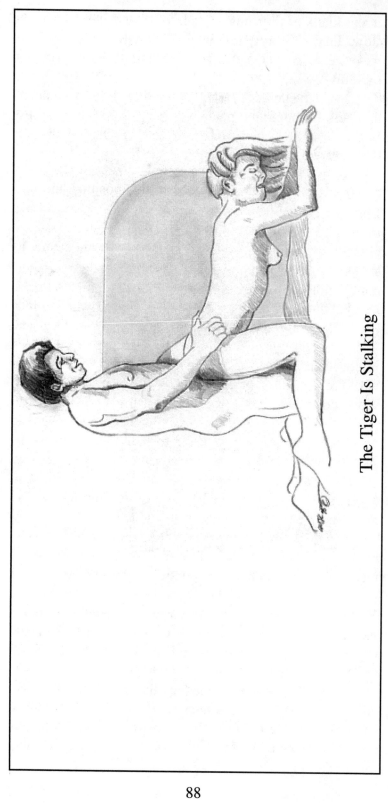

The Tiger Is Stalking

Yo-Eko, you will be on your hands and knees, and Jim, you will kneel behind her and hold her hips. Then you will insert your penis slowly but deeply inside her vagina. Pull her towards you at the same time as you thrust firmly into her for maximum penetration. Remember to feel and listen to her to make this very intimate. The thrusting of your penis should be repeated until she is completely satisfied."

Women like to feel the closeness between the vagina and the penis that is obtained in this position and men enjoy the primal feeling it can provide. The man acts like an animal approaching his mate from behind as if not intending to disturb her, but once he inserts his penis, he grabs her. Now he has control.

There are a few reasons why many men prefer this position. One is that the man can have the visual pleasures of seeing the female buttocks and body from behind, which prove most stimulating. Another is that he is free to use his hands to caress her breasts, stimulate her clitoris or control his movements by pulling the woman from behind so they can enjoy deeper penetration. He can also shake her in order to increase mutual stimulation. And yet another reason is that direct stimulation of the G-spot can be achieved with this position.

After the foreplay Yo-Eko got on her knees and I slowly entered her vagina from the rear. Her vagina was not as wet as before, but it was warm and very soft. I noticed the feeling was not all there and this made me angry. I started thrusting hard into her vagina. Master Hsu told me to grab her buttocks and give her the full length of my penis in and out. Then he directed me to place my hands on her shoulders and pull her toward me, while thrusting into her.

She came alive. Master Hsu placed my hands a little lower down her back and then back up. The angle of my penis would change according to where I put my hands. Yo-Eko loved these different angles and soon orgasmed, falling on the bed, with me on top of her. I slowly withdrew and held her softly while she rested. Yo-Eko turned and looked into my eyes. She put her arms around me and said, "Thank you."

Master Hsu left for a while and when he returned, Yo-Eko and I were still holding each other. The look in her eyes was different than earlier. She seemed contented and happy now. We looked at each other and felt very close.

Master Hsu explained the next position. It was called **The Monkey Springs**. "Yo-Eko, you lie back with your legs straight up in the air. Jim, you will kneel and rest Yo-Eko's legs on your shoulders. With her vagina fully exposed in this position you can insert your penis more easily and thrust more deeply. The thrusting of your penis in this position will stimulate her clitoris at the same time ." He also said this position could be performed with her lying on the edge of the bed and me standing in front of her.

The advantage of this position is that the vagina is clearly exposed making sexual intercourse easier and deeper. This is particularly good for a woman whose genitals are located in a lower position, and also good for a man whose penis is short or small. This position is recommended for sexual intercourse between a slim woman and a large man, because the belly of a large man often prevents him from achieving a deep penetration.

It seemed that Yo-Eko really didn't want to prolong this lovemaking session with foreplay. I sensed this and directly raised her legs on to my shoulders. Master Hsu said nothing. I wondered if I was going too fast, but he didn't say anything so I continued. My penis was already hard so I gently moved it into her luscious vagina. Slowly, circling my pelvis and thrusting side to side, I pulled her as close as I could. I could feel the heat of her moist vagina against my body. She felt so good, I began thrusting with longer strokes. Master Hsu came over and showed me how to gently bounce her up and down. When I did this Yo-Eko went wild. I barely kept up with her as she urged me to move faster and faster. She cried out in Chinese, "Don't stop! Please don't stop!" I didn't. She screamed with an intense orgasm and then we both collapsed on the bed. I kept my penis inside her while she wrapped her arms and legs around me in a tight embrace. We rested together like this for a while. It was beautiful.

About an hour later Master Hsu told us to get up and

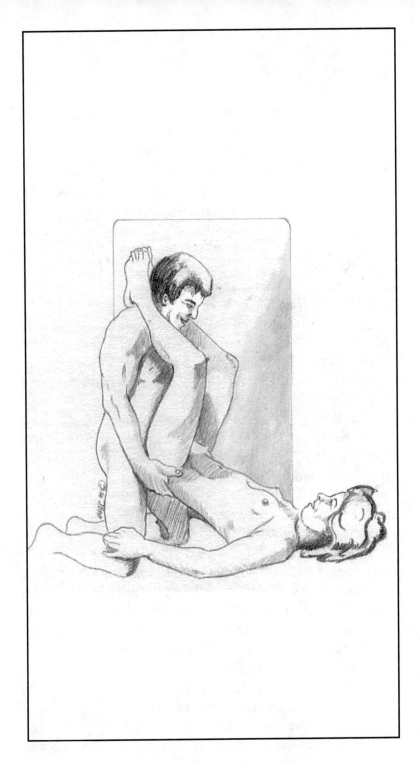

The Monkey Springs

get dressed. Yo-Eko looked at me and lovingly kissed me. Then a wonderful feeling went through my body. I was so happy I had met her! Master Hsu repeated in Chinese to get up. We did and went home.

On the way home Master Hsu didn't speak. After dinner all he said was, "Rest and I'll see you in the school at seven o'clock. I left and laid down for awhile. I thought a lot about Yo-Eko and felt happy she was my partner.

At 7:00 p.m. sharp I returned to the school and practiced kung-fu for a few hours. After practice some of the advanced students stayed, and we all drank beer, and listened to Master Hsu tell stories and jokes about different things until it was time to go home to sleep.

The next morning I was training again at 6:00 a.m. and Master Hsu came into the school and watched me. He had me do the Dragon form over and over again. This is the most grueling of Hsing-I kung-fu animal forms. It consists of jumping up in the air, while kicking scissors-like with both feet. Every once in a while he would ask me if I was tired, but I always said "No sir."

Finally he said, "Go take a shower and let's have lunch because I am tired of watching you." Inside I was very relieved as my legs were killing me and I couldn't jump much more. But I was also proud of myself as I had not given in to the overwhelming fatigue. (My previous teacher Haumea Lefiti always taught me that you never get tired, no matter what.)

After lunch Master Hsu talked more about Taoist lovemaking and he mentioned that he was concerned about Yo-Eko and me. He again explained the difference between lust and love worried that I was confusing the two. He hoped that I could finish this training. I admitted that this was harder than I had expected and that many times I wanted nothing more in the world than to ejaculate, but I promised him I would never let him down. I assured him I could endure any training. He only said, "I hope so."

A couple of days later I was back with Yo-Eko and Master Hsu explained about the next position, **The Cicada Affixed to a Tree**. He said, "This position is named after the appearance of a Cicada on a tree. Yo-Eko will lie on her

92

The Cicada Affixed to a Tree

stomach, legs straight out and buttocks raised slightly. A pillow should be placed under her stomach. Jim, you will lie on top of her back and insert your penis deeply, while lifting up her thighs slightly to stimulate her vaginal lips as you thrust into her. As you continue thrusting her secretion will increase. Be sure to watch her and notice the different stages of arousal she goes through.

This position will suit a woman whose vagina is relatively depressed and whose pubic bone is higher, thereby preventing a close touch between the vagina and the penis in a front facing position. Remember, this position is called the cicada affixed to a tree, not the cicada lying on a tree. Your weight is not to be placed directly on the back of Yo-Eko. You will be on top of her, but without throwing your full body weight on her as this could oppress her, making it difficult for her to breathe."

We started with foreplay - I loved holding Yo-Eko again. I was getting very excited kissing, holding, and caressing her body, but I controlled myself. She enjoyed it also. A few times Master Hsu told me to slow down and to put more feeling behind it. After about an hour I slowly turned Yo-Eko over, putting a pillow under her stomach, her round, firm buttocks raised high in the air. I kissed them before slowly sliding my penis in to her now moist vagina. I moved side to side thinking I had things in control when all of a sudden I had to pull out to prevent an ejaculation. "Damn," I thought, "Just when I was doing so well. The last time we met I didn't have this problem."

We rested for a few minutes and talked. The phrases "Take your mind out of your penis and put it back into your brain" and "Try to forget what you are doing and enjoy it" kept ringing in my ears. I asked Master Hsu, "How do I forget what I am doing and at the same time enjoy it?" All he said was, "You will learn with practice." So we started again. Later Master Hsu said, "OK, let's rest a while. Do you understand this position?"

The next position was called **The Tortoise Mounts**. Yo-Eko was to lie on her back and bend her knees up as I positioned myself facing her and pushed her feet with both my hands back towards her breasts. I was to insert my penis

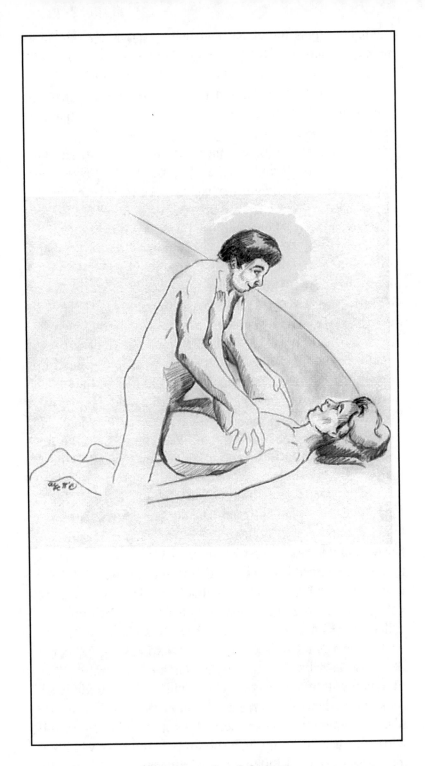

The Tortoise Mounts

slowly but deeply inside her, using deep and shallow thrusts. Master Hsu said that the movement of my penis should be moderate, repeatedly caressing the clitoris.

This position should be good for those men who take pleasure in viewing the woman's vagina as it has the unique advantage of exposing it fully to his sight.

Since Yo-Eko's vagina was already moist, she lay down on her back and let me raise her knees toward her lovely breasts. I thought her vagina looked very beautiful as I inserted my penis all the way inside her, her feet in my hands, pushing her knees higher. "Take your time," Master Hsu interrupted, "Pull out and start again." This time I went in very slowly, a little at a time, moving my pelvis in different directions. I loved this. As I began to move faster and faster, Yo- Eko pleaded, "Please, don't come." That was a mistake! Her words slammed into me having the opposite effect she had hoped for. I had to pull out right away to avoid ejaculating. I immediately bent over and sucked up my pelvic floor muscles as hard as I could to stop the semen from coming out, the way Master Hsu had taught me. Inside I was wondering, "Why can't I ejaculate just one time?" Yo-Eko looked frustrated, sad, pained, and disappointed. I thought to myself, "I'm so sorry, but I couldn't help it!"

Master Hsu went outside so I tried to apologize to Yo-Eko. She managed a smile and said, "It's all right, I know it's all part of the learning." That was when I asked her for her address so I could write to her when I went back home. She consented and wrote it down for me.   After a few minutes Master Hsu came back in. He said, "We are going to try something different with the next position. It is called **The Phoenix Flutters.**" Phoenixes are considered to be lovebirds in Chinese lore. The expression, "Phoenix Flutters" describes loving couples that are inseparable. "Yo-Eko, you will lie flat on your back, with a pillow under your back and with your legs raised slightly off the bed. Jim, you will put yourself between her thighs and support yourself with your hands. Your penis should penetrate her vagina to its deepest point. While he is inserting his penis, Yo-Eko, you should squeeze your legs together and move your hips.

96

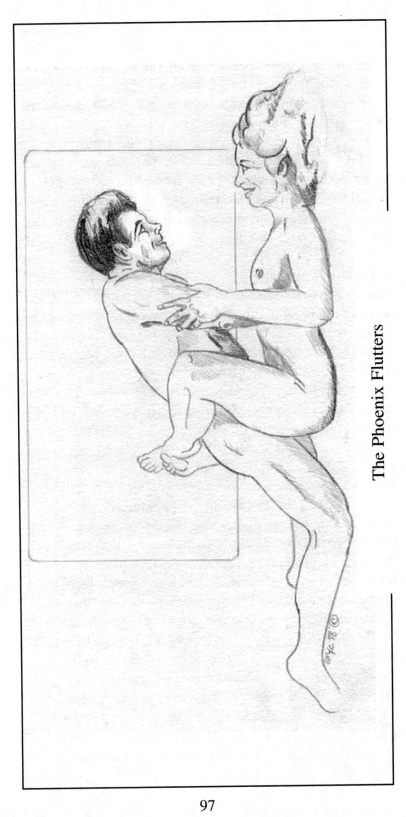

The Phoenix Flutters

97

Close your legs in an effort to tighten up your vagina and squeeze his penis as hard as you can to bring about ejaculation. The only thing is, Jim, I want you to move only your penis inside her, without moving your hips, and to think about ejaculation, but be sure to withdraw before you reach the point of no return".

Yo-Eko lay down on her back with a pillow under her and as I entered her. She squeezed her vagina, grabbing me with her vicelike grip. She was amazingly strong! I moved the best I could and thought about ejaculating, so of course, I soon had to pull out. We waited a while and Master Hsu explained how this training would help me learn to control my ejaculation. We started again and again and again. We did this for what seemed like hours. However, I soon became aware that I could stay in longer and longer. Even if I thought about ejaculating, I didn't. I wanted to move faster and with longer strokes, since it felt so good, but then Yo-Eko said she had to stop because she was getting sore. Master Hsu said it was time to go anyway.

This was my last visit with Yo-Eko because in a few days I would fly home. I turned to say good-bye and as I looked at her, tears welled in my eyes. Master Hsu said he would go outside and wait. We kissed and held each other. I really didn't want to leave, but I had to. I told her I loved her. "I'll miss you too," she said. Then we parted.

Back in the United States I continued my kung-fu training and practised the lovemaking techniques I had learned with my girlfriend. Master Hsu came to visit me in the summer of 1980 and trained me further in the higher levels of kung-fu. He stayed for about a month then, later that year, in October, I made my third visit to Taiwan. I

 spent some time training and participating in the Tang-So-Tao kung-fu tournament. I didn't do any further training in Taoist lovemaking for a week or so because there were many students from around the world competing in the tournament and Master Hsu was very busy.

One day Master Hsu came to me and said, "Take a shower, then we will eat

and go out for the afternoon." I wasn't sure where we were going. Master Hsu didn't say and I had learned not to ask.

We rode a motor scooter to the same hotel we had been at the previous year in downtown Taipei. As stated earlier, I expected to see Yo-Eko, but instead met another beautiful young woman named Mei-Tsu. I was surprised and saddened because I had looked forward to spending more time with Yo-Eko. However, I reminded myself that I was here to learn, not to fall in love.

Master Hsu wanted to see what I remembered, so we started from the beginning. I held Mei-Tsu with as much feeling as I could. Slowly I slipped off her clothes and caressed her perfect body. I was getting very turned on with Mei-Tsu, but I noticed that she was not getting as excited as I had hoped. She was different. Her kissing, her feel and her movements were all different from Yo-Eko. I couldn't figure it out. I was getting frustrated and annoyed at myself. Why is she so different? Back in the States I thought I was getting to be pretty good in lovemaking, but now I was finding out I had much more to learn.

We started sexual intercourse. I inserted my penis very slowly, one inch at a time like Master Hsu had taught me. After twenty minutes or so I pulled out again because I was about to ejaculate. We tried again and again. Sometimes I had to pull out after only ten minutes and other times we lasted until our muscles ached. Then Master Hsu said it was time to go.

A few days later we met with Mei-Tsu again and Master Hsu taught me another position called **The Rabbit Licking Its Fur**. Master Hsu turned to Mei-Tsu and said, "Jim will lie on his back with his legs straight out in front of him, and you will be on top of him, facing his feet. Put your legs on either side of his body and bend slightly forward." He then turned to me and said, "Mei-Tsu will support herself with both hands. In this position she is in complete control, while you, Jim, become the spectator. Mei-Tsu, your movements must be slow and gentle in the beginning, for in this position, as its name implies, you resemble a rabbit relaxing and licking it's fur."

Most often men have very "yang" sexual fantasies

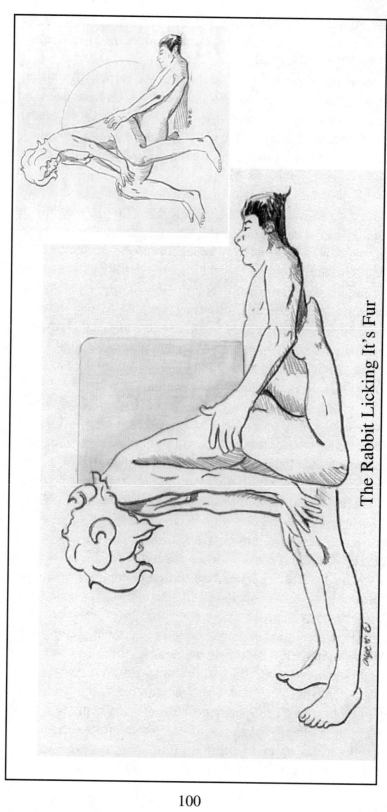

The Rabbit Licking It's Fur

of being powerful and superior, but sometimes they prefer the excitement of sex in its softer, more "yin" aspect. This love position is very suitable for aggressive women who enjoy engaging in powerful female movements to offset conventional male dominance.

The reason that this position is called Rabbit Licking Its Fur is self evident as the woman bends her knees and her head just like a rabbit licking itself. This is a sharp contrast to the Dragon Turns, as it gives superiority to the woman.

In the position of Rabbit Licking Its Fur, the man may use his hands to fondle and caress any part of the woman's body, including her hips, breasts, and waist, while the woman moves her hips up and down or side to side. Depending on the movements of the woman and the positioning of her body, the G-spot can also be stimulated with the penis, especially if she leans back. If a couple is not familiar with this position, the penis may easily slide out which is again why the woman should act like a rabbit, and go slowly and gently in the beginning.

Mei-Tsu and I slowly kissed and caressed each other. She was a cheerful person and it was a different kind of fun making love to her. I did very much enjoy kissing and touching her body, licking her sweet and beautiful vagina and fondling her lovely breasts. She soon became very excited and her vagina dripped around her rock-hard clitoris. I knew she was ready to have me enter her. She started kissing my toes and before I knew it she was lowering herself onto my penis.

I loved lying on my back and watching her slowly ride me. It seemed she had only just gotten on when she leaned backward then forward, sighed, smiled and rolled off. I reached for her as she turned to nestle into my arms. Master Hsu said, "Rest for a while and I will be back."

Later we tried the same position again. Mei-Tsu was on top looking down and moving quickly. It wasn't long before I had to pull out, because I was losing control. We started over again and again. Each time Mei-Tsu moved up, down and around using any combination of movements she could think of to bring me to orgasm. Every once in a while she would glance over her shoulder with this cute little smile on her face daring me to endure her pillow skills.

Now it was time to try the next position. Master Hsu called it **The Fish with Scales Joined**. "Jim, you will lie on your back again as in Rabbit Licking Its Fur, however this time, Mei-Tsu will be facing you and it is again she who will decide upon the movement needed to achieve orgasm. You will be able to touch and caress almost all parts of her body. You can either lie still while she controls the rhythm and depth of your penis or you can arch your back off the bed as high as you can. This will give a deeper and different angle of penetration. This position is the easiest one in which to maintain ejaculation control."

I laid on my back with my erection coming up very fast while Mei-Tsu sat slowly on my penis. She smiled that cute little smile of hers and made little gestures of pleasure with her lips. She moved faster and faster, leaning back and forth, rubbing her clitoris and playing with her breasts. I raised my body into an arch with my shoulders on the bed while pushing off on my toes. I could feel the delicious depth of her vagina and her vaginal lips rubbing over me. She orgasmed with a sigh and relaxed, but Master Hsu yelled at her to keep moving. Perspiration flowed off her dripping on to me, but she kept going. I thought she wanted badly to stop and rest, but suddenly she began gyrating fiercely, and cried out as an even more intense orgasm seized her body. She surrendered herself to the waves of energy sweeping through her and rested on top of me. This time Master Hsu let her rest.

We met Mei-Tsu again at the hotel a couple of days later and she smiled when she saw us. We talked together a while about Taoist Lovemaking and its many virtues. Master Hsu then explained about the next position, **The Cranes with Necks Intertwined**. "Jim, you will sit on your knees and Mei-Tsu will straddle your thighs, kneeling down on top of you with her legs open. She will hold you around the neck using both her hands while you insert your penis from below. Your hands will embrace her buttocks, and assist her movements. This position provides great stimulation to both partners, but a man must be physically

102

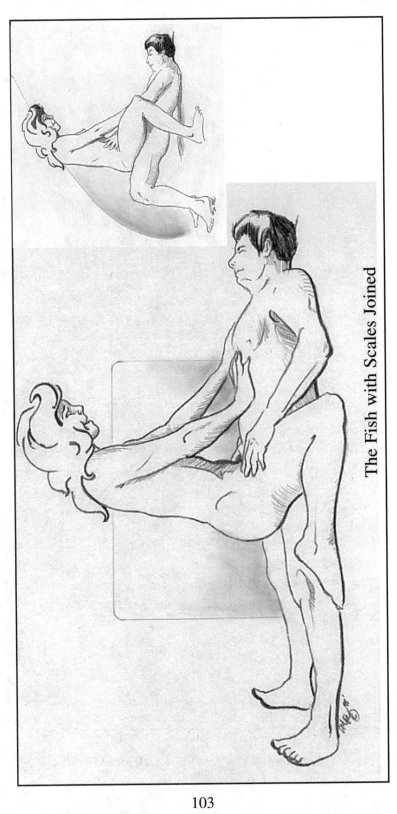

The Fish with Scales Joined

The Cranes with Necks Intertwined

fit to maintain this position for any length of time."

We started our lovemaking. I held her softly, slowly kissing her lips, face, ears, and nose. I caressed her hair, her back, and her shoulders. Ever so lightly, my fingertips brushed her skin and shivers ran through her as I tried to read her desire. When it was time, I slowly sat up, and still holding her, got on my knees as she straddled my thighs allowing my hard penis to slowly slide into the warmth of her wet vagina. She wrapped her arms around my neck squeezing us together so her firm breasts and hard nipples pressed against me. I clutched her buttocks and lifted her gently as she moved up and down. As we moved together we continued kissing each other. It was exquisite. She did not have an orgasm and neither did I, but the beauty of holding, feeling and kissing each other in this way was as profound as any orgasm we had ever had.

Later, we talked about this feeling and how powerful it was. We discussed the different types of orgasms there were, and the many virtues of Taoist lovemaking.

We continued with the last technique, **Bear Shaking the Tree**. "This is an advanced position", said Master Hsu. "In this one you will stand and hold Mei-Tsu under her buttocks. Her feet will be wrapped around your waist, and her arms around your neck. You will move your hips forward and backwards and Mei-Tsu will respond to your movements. This position allows for very deep penetration and an enhanced closeness of your body that will stimulate her clitoris. She will truly love this position. Mei-Tsu, it will help Jim if you push down hard on his shoulders with your arms as he is holding you."

As in the last position, this is best practiced by couples who are physically fit.

We started kissing and holding each other again. Master Hsu instructed Mei-Tsu to get on top of me and a few minutes later, he told me to stand up as she held tightly on to me. As I stood up, my penis slid deeper inside her and she moaned with pleasure. I continued lifting her up and down with my hands while moving my hips back and forth. Mei-Tsu gasped and sighed as her orgasm swept over her. As we fell to the bed to rest Mei-Tsu stayed on top of

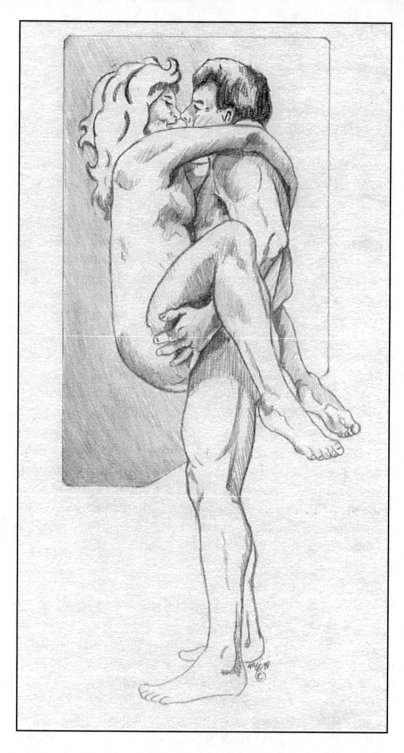

The Bear Shaking the Tree

me with my penis still inside her and her head resting on my shoulder.

After a while, we got up and dressed and Mei-Tsu asked Master Hsu if we could get together again soon. He just smiled and said, "I'll call you when we know." She gave me a very deep kiss and said in Chinese, "Thank you very much."

With only about a week to go before I had to go back to the States, I didn't know if we were going to have time to practice again. I had learned so much during this visit to Taiwan. Each trip was revealing more of the wonders of lovemaking to me.

COMBINING THE TEN WAYS

One afternoon after lunch, Master Hsu told me that he was going to teach me the last of the positions. I really didn't know what he was talking about because we had gone through all of them. So I asked him, "Are there more? I thought we had finished the ten positions." He smiled and said, "You'll see."

We met with Mei-Tsu again, and I could see that she was prepared to be fully satisfied. Master Hsu reviewed the ten ways that we had been practicing, the merits of each one and said how after mastering the positions, couples should vary them, moving from one to the next, but without having to withdraw the penis. "Keep in mind however", he said, "That an orgasm is not ejaculation. An orgasm can last as long as you want and can travel as high as you want but once the man has ejaculated, the orgasm is gone. The most pleasurable time is the peak of orgasm right before ejaculation. During your lovemaking, practice bringing each other to the highest peak possible, then back to a lower relaxed level. In this way, you will be able to exchange the energies of Yin and Yang with each other and remain in complete harmony for an extended period of time."

We started making love, and thinking this was the last time I would see Mei-Tsu, I put everything into it. I tried harder than ever before. After about an hour of foreplay, she was very excited. She orgasmed twice while I tongued her lovely vagina. Then, we started into the first position, **The Dragon Turns**, with Mei-Tsu lying on her back. I laid on top of her using the nine shallow and one

deep technique, as well as the other different methods of thrusting and angles of penetration.

I heard a voice behind me say "change to **Cranes With Necks Intertwined**. I leaned back and pulled Mei-Tsu up on to my lap as I kneeled down. She held on around my neck with both hands, keeping my penis inside her. My hands embraced her buttocks and assisted her movements up and down.

After a while Master Hsu told us to change to **Fish With Scales Joined**". I moved onto my back, still keeping my penis inside her vagina, and pulled her on top of me. Now she was in complete control. She started

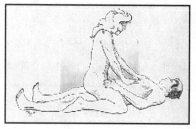

moving slowly at first then faster. My penis was hitting her G- spot and she moved faster and faster until she orgasmed. By this time she was exhausted, leaning on top of me, resting.

Master Hsu next had us move to **Phoenix Flutters**. We hugged each other and rolled over until Mei-Tsu was again lying on her back underneath me. She wrapped her legs around me and squeezed tightly. I fluttered my penis inside her without moving my pelvis. She smiled her approval and said that it felt very good.

As she released her legs I moved my pelvis in different directions.

Then Master Hsu had us go to **The Monkey Springs**. Since Mei-Tsu was already on her back I simply

changed the position of her legs, without withdrawing my penis, by raising them up onto my shoulders. I grabbed the lower part of her thighs and started moving her up and down, my penis deep inside her. Her clitoris was rubbing on my body and soon she was begging me not to stop and she was overcome with yet another orgasm.

I lowered her legs into The Dragon Turns position so that she could rest while still keeping my penis deep inside her vagina.

The Tortoise Mounts was the next position that Master Hsu had us move into. I raised her legs up and pushed her knees toward her breasts. Using deep and shal-

low strokes, and shaking her knees back and forth, I could see Mei-Tsu was coming back to life. "I like this position too, I like them all. Oh please let's never stop, this is so beautiful!" she exclaimed.

Then Master Hsu said to move into **Bear Shaking the Tree**. I slowly lowered her legs and put my hands under her buttocks as she wrapped her arms and legs around me. I stood up

and started moving my hips forward and backward. Mei-Tsu clutched me and moaned with delight and I shook her up and down on my hard penis as deeply as I could. I laid Mei-Tsu back down on the bed and now we were back to Fish With Scales Joined.

Although Master Hsu continued to instruct us, I became less and less aware of his presence and more aware of the connection between Mei-Tsu and myself.

I wasn't too sure how to change into the next position which was to be **Rabbit Licking It's Fur**, but I thought to myself, "This ought to be good." Mei-Tsu liked this one

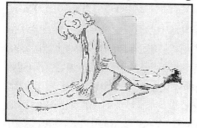

and started to get into position. Master Hsu said, "Lift one foot over him as you are turning and be careful not to let his penis out of your vagina." Now she was facing my feet and started moving fast, leaning back so my penis could rub against her G-spot.

Next Master Hsu had us change to **The Tiger Stalking**. Mei-Tsu leaned forward and got on her knees and I did the same, being careful to hold her close so that my

penis would not slip out. I looked at her beautiful round buttocks, grabbed her hips and started thrusting in and out going as deeply as I could, hitting her G spot. The perspiration was flow-

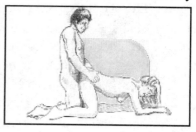

ing from both our bodies. She was loving it and so was I. "Please don't stop," she gasped and another orgasm enveloped her.

Next came **The Cicada Affixed To A Tree**. She lowered her body down as I continued to thrust at her G-spot, but Mei-Tsu was exhausted and couldn't enjoy this

position. Master Hsu saw this and had us roll on our sides and just hold each other. Mei-Tsu soon fell into a sweet sleep while I held her. Master Hsu left the room as we rested.

When he returned we got dressed. The next time I saw Master Hsu he said, "Now you have a better understanding of the Taoist ways of loving and of how sex can greatly contribute to the fulfillment of your life. Do not forget all that I have taught you. Conserve your semen, as it is your most precious possession and be sure always to fully satisfy your partner thereby allowing you both to find the infinite harmony of yin and yang. If you remember these things you may continue your lovemaking all night long, cultivating and preserving your inner energy. This will keep you young and healthy for a long time. Without this basic harmony of yin and yang, neither medicines nor herbs will be of any use to you. Train hard and practice as much as you can. Do not underestimate the importance and power of what you have learned. You must live the way of the Tao. You are very fortunate to have learned all this and you know what my feelings are for you as my student. What I have handed down to you has been passed down to me from my teacher and his teachers before him, all the way back to the reign of Huang Ti the Yellow Emperor of China. One day you will find someone to whom you will pass on this knowledge as it has been passed on for these last 4000 years."

Chapter 10

CULTIVATION OF SEXUAL ENERGY

Between Partners

It was during Master Chiao's second visit to the United States that I learned about cultivation of sexual energy between partners. One night after we had reviewed all the things he had previously taught me, Master Chiao talked about yin and yang and how these apparently separate, contrary forces combined to create an ultimate unity or harmony and were therefore necessary to each other. He said, "The Taoists believed that in order for man (yang) to be nourished he requires the assistance of woman (yin) and vice versa. By absorbing the yin and yang from each other during sex, it is possible to nourish the energy of self. By cultivating sexual energy through sexual meditation, good health and longevity are favored. Without this nourishment one's health and longevity will be negatively affected.

By understanding these ideas of Yin and Yang, your ideas about the use of sexual intercourse will change and you will learn to open yourself completely to your partner. In this form of meditation, ejaculation is not deliberately sought. By not ejaculating, your sexual energies are allowed to circulate and become one with your lover's. Pleasure and ecstasy will fill your bodies as sexual energy is exchanged over and over again.

"I will teach both you and your partner, Melinda, how to circulate each other's sexual energy through the large and small Little Nine Heaven circles. During this type of meditation you both must recite at specific times the mantras that I will teach you. These are not to be given to anyone else." Master Chiao then instructed me to sit down on a hard pad and had my partner Melinda sit on top of me with my penis inside her vagina.

"In solo meditation, the tongue acts as a bridge in your own body by connecting the two channels to form one, but in the practice of circulating energy between you and Melinda, the genitals act as the bridge. Your sexual energy follows the route of the Functional channel down to the genitals where it then crosses over to Melinda's genitals and continues along the upward path of her Governor channel. In this way a continuous path of energy is maintained between the both of you. By this process you and Melinda will experience a form of meditation which is deeply shared and can be enjoyed without losing any of your life force energy. Most importantly, you both will gain a new sense of inner satisfaction that will be with both of you long after the sexual pleasure has become only a memory. At these advanced levels, you and she will be taught to re- circulate your sexual energies."

Melinda and I practiced this style of sexual meditation for one hour at least four times a week for several years.

Master Chiao learned this system of sexual energy from his teacher, Elder Kong-Ka, the first person to operate a Me-Tsu religion temple in Taiwan. She passed away on April 11, 1997 at 108 years of age! It was her death wish to have her corpse preserved for three years. After that, her body shall be made into a "Buddha in the flesh" for her disciples to worship. The only words that she left for her students and disciples were that they should continue their practice.

Higher Level of Sexual Meditation

In 1985 while I was in Taiwan practicing kung-fu and meditation with Master Chiao, he told me of even more advanced levels of meditation. Here couples can practice an exchange of sexual energy without actually touching each other. He said, "To begin with, two partners must love each other very much and this method will nourish and deepen the love that is between them."

He told me, "Sit across the room facing your partner. You should feel aroused by her presence. By focusing your minds on the aura of each other and opening your bodies to allow sexual energy to enter, you both will be able to achieve the pleasures of sexual intercourse without the physical contact."

When I got back home to California, Melinda and I practiced this style of meditation as often as we could, however we were never able to fully achieve this highest level of meditation to our satisfaction.

Sexual Vampirism

In sexual vampirism one partner drains the other's sexual energy or life force. I have heard many stories of old Taoist men who seek out young childless women as sexual partners, for their abundant Yin energy. This has been practiced for many generations in select Taoist circles, where an older man will hire a young woman to be his lover for a specific period of time, usually one month or so, for the sole purpose of acquiring her yin energy for his own benefit. This can be very harmful to the woman, but if he is a kind man she will be handsomely rewarded and given herbs to ensure her full recovery. However, countless stories tell of Taoist men and women who have abused others with this technique and become very powerful. A woman who masters this system can be even more dangerous than any man, for a woman can drain a man's energy many times faster than a man can drain a woman's.

Even when assuming no evil intentions, the draining of a partner's energy can happen unintentionally. Most often this occurs if only one partner knows the practice. The safeguard against this is to circulate the energy through both partners' bodies. This exchange of energy eliminates the possibility of one partner gaining energy while the other one loses it.

After I learned about sexual vampirism, Melinda wanted me to drain her of her energy just to see what it felt like. I told her it wasn't good to do this very often, but she wanted very much to feel it. As we practiced, I tried and tried to drain her energy. She had waves of orgasms, but that was all. But we knew there could be more. I kept trying to perfect myself and we practiced continually. After six months, during a practice, she suddenly began to lose her energy. I kept drawing it from her as much as I could. I began to feel very strong; an invincible feeling, that nothing could hurt me. Then she panicked. Multiple orgasms swept over her and her strength vanished with each orgasm. She was scared, yet wanted to take it a little further. I quickly realized she had gone far enough so I stopped draining her and held her softly while I gave her back her energy through a special technique Master Chiao had taught me. Within seconds she was better.

Later she told me of her fear of dying mixed with the ecstasy of intense orgasms. The pleasure and fear excited and terrified her, but she knew I would keep her safe. She wanted to do it more and more, but I knew the danger it could cause so I would rarely agree to do it.

If you find yourself with a partner who knows the

116

technique of vampirism, or draining another's energy, there is really nothing you can do to protect yourself should he or she choose to use you in this way. Fortunately, people who are truly capable of doing this are not very common, but be aware that this is possible, and again, I emphasize the need for good communication.

EPILOGUE

"The years will see what the days will never know."
-Old Chinese saying.

Having been on this unexpected journey and learning how to generate, cultivate and direct sexual energy toward spiritual realization has made my life richer and fuller than I ever imagined possible. I will say again that it is my sincere hope that you too will gain a lifetime of benefits from what I have learned. Let me remind you that the goal is to develop yourself to your fullest potential and live the entire course of your life fully and well. Do the exercises - you won't regret it. Learn to really listen to and hear each other so that you can respond accordingly not only during lovemaking but in all aspects of relationship. Enjoy the fruits of your effort and give thanks. Share the good feelings and energy you create for the benefit of others. This is the true meaning of "making love."

Remember that it is necessary to be cautious when engaging in a new sexual relationship. Inform yourself of the dangers that exist in the form of AIDS and other sexually transmitted diseases and be intelligent about your lovemaking by taking the necessary precautions.

Don't be discouraged if you do not get immediate results from the exercises but know that with steady effort over the weeks and months, progress will come in leaps and bounds. There will be times when you feel that nothing is happening or changing even though you are practicing hard. Don't give up and continue your practice as there will come a day when suddenly you will notice a big difference. Do not underestimate the effectiveness of these simple exercises.

Keep in mind what you are hoping to achieve. Set your goal, however lofty and distant it may seem and dedicate all your energy generated by lovemaking and everything else you do, toward the realization of that goal.

Almost every man and woman has the ability to have sex like every animal of almost every species. But as humans we have the ability to not just have sex, but to feel and love and enjoy the beauty of orgasm and ejaculation. The human body is equipped with many nerve endings, so why not learn to fully engage these and develop the senses with which we are endowed and make sex beautiful? Why not learn not only to have good sex, but to make love while doing it.

There is nothing more wonderful than after making love to look into your loved one's eyes and see them sparkle and shine with beauty, happiness and fulfillment and to then tell her or him, "I love you. Good night."

Could the Ancient Knowledge of Shih-Shui Kung-Fu be the Fountain of Youth?

From ancient to modern times, men and women have always sought out ways to live healthier and longer lives. There is a Taoist training called Shih-Shui which in the past was kept largely secret and taught only to a few Taoist monks as an effective source of rejuvenation and a way to enlightenment. Practitioners of Shi-Shui enjoy many benefits including enhanced sexual power and pleasure, better control of ejaculation for men, tighter vaginal muscles for women, and the ability to prolong love-making for as long as desired. It has been proven to also dramatically improve immune functioning. The overall benefits to the body and mind can be summarized as "Harder, Stronger, Longer."

The world's leading expert in Shih-Shui is Master Chiao Chang-Hung. He is the 33rd generation of the Little Nine Heaven Internal Kung-Fu system. The style consists of Ju Kung (boxing), Chian Kuan-Jen (swordsmanship) and Shih Shui Kung (bone marrow washing). Master Chiao learned the Little Nine Heaven system from the high priest of the Taoist temple on Lu Mountain in the District of Jing-Zhou, Shenyang Province, China.

The Taoists believe that life may be extended by individual effort and is not solely controlled by nature. In Shih-Shui, the internal body is exercised. Most people are familiar with external power that is generated by the external movements of the body and muscles. Internal power, however, is more complex in that it involves the internal organs and the circulatory and nervous systems.

Shih-Shui is a method of attaining health and longevity, for both men and women, through sexual vitality. Scientists have found that some hormones (DHEA-sulphate in particular) directly control the aging process and ultimately, life itself. Shih-Shui is a method by which one can fully extract the essence of vital energy from the gonads that produce this hormone and use it to preserve and extend life.

The doctrine of the Taoist arts states that "To preserve or provide is at my will." This implies that the human body possesses a mechanism for self-preservation and a very potent healing ability. The Shih-Shui practitioner can even develop the ability to control reproduction at will rather than resort to surgical operations.

During the first stage, the practitioner learns the testicle/ovary exercises, which stimulate hormone generation. He or she is then taught how to reverse the flow of gonad secretions to the brain. Through special internal exercises the sexual essence is then channeled to the limbs to nourish and improve the health of the entire body. This helps to prevent aging of the physical body and to eliminate illness associated with old age.

By mastering the Shih-Shui exercises one is able to cultivate and increase intrinsic energy and experience love making that was before unobtainable and unimaginable.

James W. McNeil is Master Chiao Chang-Hung's only American student who is qualified and licensed to teach the Shih-Shui training.

James McNeil is demonstrating a small but important part of the Shih Shui training by swinging over two hundred pounds with his genitals. Melinda is lifting 5 pounds with her vaginal muscles.

About the Author

James W. McNeil was born in 1942 in the small town of Webster Groves, Missouri, where he lived with his brothers and grandparents. In 1954 he moved to California and lived near the famous Chinatown district of Los Angeles where he began what would become a very extensive education in a diversity of martial arts:

1966-1973: Studied under Haumea (Tiny) Lefiti. Obtained the highest degree black belt given at that time for Splashing Hands fighting techniques.

1973-1977: Studied under Sifu Ralph Shunn the Shaolin Five Animals, Wing Chun, Iron Hand and received extensive training in all weapons. Obtained the rank of head instructor in June, 1976.

1977-1984: Studied under Master Hsu Hong-Chi in Taipei, Taiwan. Received extensive training in the arts of Chi-Kung and Hsing-I. Also was taught Tui-Na, Acupressure Massage, Taoist Sexual Techniques, and Meditation.

Obtained a 4th degree black belt in Hsing-I in 1983.

1984-1997: Studied under Chin Chen-Yen in Taipei, Taiwan. Trained in the Tzu Men-Chuan system and advanced Iron Hand techniques.

1983-1997: Studied under Master Pan Wing-Chow in Taipei, Taiwan. Trained in the original style of Chen Tai-Chi.

In addition to his training in Taoist Lovemaking and martial arts James McNeil has completed a one year program in Chinese Psychic Healing with Hsu Ting-Ming at the Psychic Research Institute of Taiwan in 1987. He was also awarded a Doctorate in Clinical Hypnotherapy from the American Institute of Hypnotherapy in 1990.

Since 1984 James McNeil has been a student of **Master Chiao Chang-Hung,** of Taipei, Taiwan. He is currently receiving advanced training in Taoist sexual techniques and "Little Nine Heaven" Kung-Fu which consists of ju kung (fighting), chian-kuan jen (swordsmanship), and Shih-Shui (bone marrow washing). He is also being taught advanced Pa-Kua, and Hsing-I and is receiving further training in the higher levels of Chi-Kung, Nei-Kung and meditation.

Little Nine Heaven Internal Kung-Fu Retreat Center

Several years ago Master Chiao expressed his wish to see a training center established where the Little Nine heaven system could be taught in the traditional manner, in the spirit of the ancient Taoist temples. James McNeil has created such a center consisting of a training hall and full residential facilities for students, amidst the beautiful mountains and citrus orchards of Rainbow, California. When he is not travelling the world teaching seminars it is here that he conducts his 4-12 week long intensive training sessions in the fighting, healing and spiritual arts of ancient China.

James W. McNeil is author of the following:

Books

    1. <u>Hsing-I:</u> Unique Publication, Inc., 1993

    2. <u>Ancient Lovemaking Secrets - The Journey Toward Immortality:</u> L9H Publication, 1998.

COMING IN 1999.....

    3. <u>Little Nine Heaven Kung-Fu: The Oldest Taoist System Known Today:</u> L9H Publication.

    4. <u>The Unity Between the Tao-Teh-Ching and Tai-Chi:</u> L9H Publication

    5. The Continuing Journing Toward Immortality. L9H Publication

Videos

    1. Chinese Lovemaking Secrets: Part 1& 2

    2. Hsing-I Internal Kung-Fu (10 video set)

    3. Chi-Kung Acupressure for Health

    4. Ancient Chinese Art Of Tui-Na

    5. Staff Form (weapon)

    6. Tien Gunn (Chi-Kung video): Parts 1 & 2

    7. Butterfly Knives Form (weapon)

    8. Eight Section Brocade (Chi-Kung video)

    9. Splashing Hands Kung-Fu Parts 1 & 2 (fighting)

    10. Chen Tai-Chi: Parts 1 & 2

    11. Iron Hand Training

For More Information

For general information or for details on specific programs (including Hsing-I, Splashing Hands, Chen Tai-Chi, Shih-Shui, Tui-Na, Acupressure Massage, Chi-Kung, Meditation, Pa-Kua, Iron Hand Training and Taoist Lovemaking), for seminars and training schedules, and to order books and videos please contact Sifu James McNeil at:

Little Nine Heaven Internal Kung-Fu
1257 Rainbow Valley Blvd.,
Rainbow, CA 92028
USA
Phone: (760) 731-1416
Fax: (760) 728-3792

www.ftos.net/heavenkungfu

For those who are interested, the following books are recommended for futher reading :

1. Shih Shui Kung (Bone Marrow Washing), Master Chiao Chang-Hung. (In Chinese)

2. The Tao Of Sex, Akira Ishihara & Howard Levy.

3. The Yellow Emperor's Classic of Internal Medicine, Ilza Veith.

4. The Tao Of Love & Sex, Jolan Chang.

5. Tao-Teh-Ching, Lao-tzu.